WHY CAN'T I GET OVER KA✦RINA?

The Greatest Disaster Ever MADE

Zelia E. Williams

Published by Godzchild Publications
a division of Godzchild, Inc.
22 Halleck St., Newark, NJ 07104
www.godzchildproductions.net

Printed in the United States of America 2011— First Edition

Special thanks to:
University of Wisconsin-Madison
Space Science & Engineering Center ~ Hurricane cover image

Cover Design & Back Cover Photograph
Kaylan-Torey Brown

Editors
Reverend Ellis Williams
Debra W. Lucas
Debra Watson

ISBN 978-1-9370950-9-3 (pbk.)

For information about special discounts for bulk purchases, please contact Godzchild
Inc. at (877) 777-7016 or _godzchildinc@gmail.com_. Also, for information on having the
author speak at your live event, book club, or organization, visit our website at
www.whycantigetoverkatrina.com.

2011000000

This book is dedicated to my daughters
who remain focused and driven by their academic
achievements and personal accomplishments.
You are beautiful and brilliant!
Always remember that the trinity to success is a great education,
contributions to your family and community, and love and faith in Christ.
For these three things shall NEVER be taken away from you.
Special thanks and gratitude to my mom and dad,
Reverend Ellis & Priscilla N. Williams.
Your undying love and support have made me the person I am today.

TABLE OF CONTENTS

Gentrification (gen-tri-fi-ca-tion) *is the process of renewal and rebuilding accompanying the influx of middle-class or affluent people into deteriorating areas that often displaces poorer residents. First known use of gentrification was in 1964.*

Merriam-Webster Dictionary

PREFACE

FROM CLEVER MARKETING STRATEGIES TO PLACE AN African-American on television as the *face* of New Orleans and the *spokesperson* for the Louisiana Road Home Program (BP did the same thing regarding the oil spill on the Gulf Coast); behind the scenes were other groups of incompetent directors receiving multiple unimaginable salaries as we ignored the fact that a greater devastation was occurring right before our very eyes; the beginning of gentrification.

UN
THE MOVE

JUNE 25, 2005

HOTTER THAN USUAL, MOVING DAY WAS EXHAUSTING, as most moves are when you're relocating from one major city to the next. This move however, would be a familiar one, in that I was moving back to New Orleans, Louisiana (NOLA), my hometown, after living in Houston, Texas for the past four years with my two young daughters.

For years, I've always wanted to experience Houston ever since graduating from Dillard University. And after 12½ years of marriage and recently getting divorced, why not!

Filled with extraordinarily accomplished people, Houston was culturally challenged. Sometimes it was those who were too busy to simply relax. It had no flavor like back home. Houston had no parks with a lake or a breathtaking view. It had no sidewalks!

Everything closed at 2 AM. In New Orleans we're just getting started! In New Orleans, friendships are like no other. They're nurtured, they're well-regarded, and they're brotherly and sisterly. And they last for decades...or until one or the other dies! Friendships in New Orleans were synonymous with good food, fine restaurants, walks in the parks (all of them), church on Sundays, crawfish on the Lakefront, beautiful people of *all* races, drive thru Daiquiris, Wheel of Fortune, Tyler Perry, and the Ellen DeGeneres Show...local treasures!

Only in New Orleans can you stop by your girlfriend's house unannounced to get a bite to eat...and vice versa for that fact. In Houston, if you have to travel on I-59 or I-45 to get to someone's house, you can definitely count on traffic or an accident to slow you down, or stop you dead in your tracks—for hours. Back home, 15 minutes max got you just about anywhere in the City.

Having been away from family members and friends, and not having that structured support system in place was, indeed, quite the challenge. Going back home; however, and being with family would allow me the flexibility and less rigidness that was prominent in Houston.

As hot as it was that Saturday though, the first order of business when I got to New Orleans was getting a medium strawberry snowball with condensed milk from The Original New Orleans Snowballs next to Brother Martin High School on Elysian Fields Avenue. Ahhh! Good times—good times!!

Next week would be a busy week for me, as I would be preparing for my Residential Appraising course so that I could add another certification and skill set to my federal housing background and grants management profession. I couldn't have been more than excited. I had researched several leading Appraisers in New Orleans and decided that Jim Thorns of Jim Thorns Consulting was the firm that I wanted to connect with. When I was Adviser with the Mayor's Division of Housing and Neighborhood Development, Jim's office contributed a great deal.

NEW ORLEANS- Getting settled in was equally tiring. We had finally finished with unpacking all of the boxes and getting that snowball that I thought about all day. It seemed like an unusually hot summer. "Ohh, uhh-uhh,!" I thought to myself. The heat was just unbearable, and the humidity in New Orleans wasn't helping matters.

I called Juan to let him know that the girls and I had settled in and that I was looking for a school to place them in. Juan and I had been dating for almost a year. I met him in Houston at a convention last September. Out of hundreds of people in the room, there was something about his swagger. Actually, I met him in the VIP room upstairs where it was less crowded. I was there with some girlfriends and when we sat down he was coming over to our table to sit with us. Immediately, another guy took the seat Juan was attempting to get. Juan knew the girl I came to the party with and spoke to her and asked who I was. She introduced me to him and he sat at the table behind us. As I sat there talking with my girlfriend, the guy who sat next to me who took Juan's intended seat talked to me ad nauseum.

Every time I turned around, there was Juan staring at me. Juan was strikingly gorgeous! I turned sideways and crossed my legs so he could get a better view. Juan was the only guy at a table of about nine women. And he sat there just *staring* at <u>me</u>. The third time I turned around; I looked him directly in his eyes and smiled. Three seconds was all it took and the next thing I knew Juan was walking towards me as the crowd of women who astoundingly watched him walk away from them and towards me. He came over to where I was sitting and asked me if we could talk. "Oh hell yeah" I was thinking. *"Sure,"* I told him nicely. Juan extended his hand out to help me up so that we could walk to another area of the VIP room and talk in private. It was like the scene from Mahogany where I was Diana Ross and Juan was Billy Dee! We talked about everything you should never talk about when you first meet someone. We talked about religion, politics, careers, and goals. I quickly realized that education was as important to Juan as it was to me. We had an awful lot in common. Juan told me that he always wanted to get into real estate to become a developer. I told him to *"Just Do It!"* Later on, he confided in me and told me that it was <u>those three words</u> that made him realize that I was a very supportive and encouraging woman. He said he wanted desperately to get to know more about me. After we finished talking, I went back downstairs to where everyone was and danced with a fraternity brother. This frat was a good friend of mine. After our dance that same guy who was sitting next to me earlier found me, and started talking ad nauseum again—for 45 minutes. I couldn't tell you today what he talked about or why I didn't make an excuse to exit away from him. Lord knows I should have. But being a polite person, I smiled and laughed at whatever he was saying. When I saw Juan a few feet behind me, I quickly made an excuse to break away and told the guy I was leaving to go home. I then purposely backed up into Juan. Juan grabbed me and I turned around and apologized and pretended like I didn't notice him being there. He asked me if I was enjoying myself and to save a dance for him when my favorite song came on. *"My favorite song is playing right now,"* I told him as I smiled. While Juan and I danced, my frat brother kept interrupting us as if he was jealous or something. He just came over and started talking about much of nothing to the both of us while we danced. Besides the unexpected interruptions, Juan remained calm and polite. After our dance, Juan and I were headed back upstairs to the VIP room when he was approached by one of the women who sat at his table. I was approached by someone from the NBA. He asked me if he could talk to me or give me a ride home. I told the ball player that I was with some girlfriends and that I was ok on the ride. I turned around to look for Juan and he was gone. The ball player insisted again and I politely told him, *"no thanks."* As I got to the top of the stairs, Juan was already there waiting for me. He apologized for the interruption and told me, *"I see I can't leave you alone for too long...you've got players offering you a ride home."* *"Like you don't have women running all up under you,"* I told him. We talked some more until it was time to leave. He asked me if I had a ride home and we both laughed. He asked if he could have my number. It was Thursday night and I had to go to work the next day.

While I was at work, I received three unfamiliar long distance phone calls from Tennessee on my cell. When I played them back, they were all from Juan wanting to know if I was going to the rest of the party convention events that weekend. I told him I was. The Gap Band was supposed to be playing that Friday night at one of the events.

Later on that evening, Juan called me again and asked me jokingly if I was going to stand him up. I told him no but that I wouldn't be able to come that night because I felt like I was coming down with a cold or something. I really wasn't one to hang out much, and the night before I had worn a halter- top dress, and it was pretty chilly out. He asked me if I needed him to bring me anything and that he was going to be in town until Sunday. He said he really wanted to see me again. I told him that I didn't feel up to it that night but that if I felt better Saturday, I would take him out on the town to see Houston.

Saturday morning, Juan called me to see if I needed him to bring me breakfast. He definitely was a smooth guy. Wanting to see him as much as he wanted to see me, since my divorce, I really didn't feel like getting into another relationship. It had been eight years. But there was something about Juan that was uniquely refreshing. He was smart, tall, a gentleman, and eye candy too! He was like a breath of fresh air.

Saturday evening, I picked Juan up at the Four Seasons downtown. He knew he was looking *good* in those jeans! I wore a halter-top body suit with jeans and high heels. You would have thought that I would have learned from the halter-top dress that I wore two nights ago in the cold air. As I pulled up, he saw my front license plate that had the emblem of the Sorority that I'm affiliated with. He motioned his hand to cue me in on that he was my fraternity brother, as well. My, my, we did have a lot in common. We decided to take in a movie and dinner. After dinner, we went to the Mercury Room downtown until it was the last call. We then drove around town 'cause there's nowhere to go in Houston after 2 a.m. I was thinking to myself, if only we were in New Orleans, we could still be up in the club. Juan asked me if I wanted to go to the Four Seasons and come up to his room to talk some more. I drove to the hotel and parked in front. As he was getting out of my car, I grabbed his arm and asked him if we could stay in the car and talk. He promised me that if I came up to the room with him he would be the perfect gentleman and that he "wouldn't bite." It wasn't the *biting* I was worried about. Juan was a pretty big guy. He wasn't overweight, but had lots and lots of muscles. I don't think he had an ounce of body fat on him anywhere. I still wasn't completely over whatever it was that I was trying to come down with. And I wasn't in the mood to have to fight off somebody and go 9th Ward on Juan. Not that I would have fought *him* off anyway. It was 3 in the morning, and all was well with the universe. Everything was perfect... the conversation, the mood, and of course, Juan. It had been a minute since I had been with someone...actually a few years. He would have made front headlines the next day, had I gone up to the room with him. The papers would have read, *"Man at the Four Seasons Found Dead in his Room With a Smile."* Besides, I had to stick to my 90 day rule. So just in case, Juan and I stayed in my car and talked, and laughed, and kissed until 4:30 in the morning. Normally, it takes me about 90 days to find out what I need to know about someone before I do *anything* with them. As I drove home, Juan called me so that we could talk some more on the phone until I made it home safely. It was September of 2004. I will never forget the day that I met Juan.

Over the next few months, we talked on the phone 24/7 about everything. Every month, he came to see me. And three-day weekends eventually became four and five-day extended weekends. After we became an item, he came to everything and actively participated in my girl's education, school meetings, and social life. Juan was the first guy that I met who seemed to have everything or what I call the *'total package.'* He was sharp, funny, encouraging, supportive, incredibly thoughtful, 6'4", had a body like Dwayne "The Rock" Johnson, and looked like Boris Kodjoe. Cha-Ching!

Juan wanted to know what day I was planning to have Torey's party. Torey was making nine years old next month in July. Juan was the first man, besides daddy, to actually pray for me. The weekends we were together, we went to daddy's church. All the men, including the Pastor, would come over to tell him how lucky he was, but actually to really check him out. Juan was truly a lucky man, and I felt blessed to have *him* in my life. Everyone at church was surprised, yet happy, to see me with someone. As picky as I am with men, I was surprised my damn self.

Juan was a well-educated, well read intellectual; both street and book smart. Normally after 15 minutes, I can pretty much sum up someone and know whether or not if I'm interested.

An alumnus of LSU, Juan was from Detroit and five years younger than me. I was 39 and he was going to be 34 in November. I get approached by a lot of guys, and in 39 years, I had never met someone as caring and attentive as Juan. No one had sparked my interest as much as him. Unbeknownst to him, he was the *only* guy whose 15 minutes turned into an entire weekend. And one month after knowing him, the *only* guy that I abolished my 90 day rule for.

✠ ✠ ✠

That Monday, Juan's first email to me read:

From: Juan

Sent: Mon 9/20/04 11:59 AM

To: *xxxxxxxxxxxxxxx@msn.com*

You are so beautiful

Beauty:

The quality that gives pleasure to the mind or senses and is associated with such properties as harmony of form or color, excellence of artistry, truthfulness, and originality.

Gorgeous:

Dazzlingly beautiful or magnificent

Characterized by magnificence or virtuosic brilliance

Informal. Wonderful; delightful.

Having read these two definitions, you should not be surprised to hear me say that you are the most beautiful lady I have ever had the pleasure of meeting.

The fact that you are gorgeous only adds to your "TOTAL PACKAGE". Whoever stated that beauty is only skin deep was lying. Beauty starts from within and expresses itself on the outside. I am sure you know that. I am awaiting your call like an anxious 18 year old teenager waiting for a yes from the girl he asked to the prom. Are you sure the things I was told by my friends about you Louisiana girls was not true? I keep playing the whole night over and over and over. Whatever you put in my drink is working. Mission accomplished. I am thinking about you like crazy. I enjoyed the conversation. I really appreciate you listening to me talk about my goals and dreams of being an entrepreneur. Support is a really underrated quality. The support of a <u>lady</u> gives men the power to do anything. As simple as it was to hear you say "Just Do it" really capped the evening for me. Like someone once said "it's the best part."

The fact that you have a passion out of this world does not hurt either.

Again, you looked great but you know that. I appreciate your hospitality and look forward to seeing you again SOON!!

Juan

Checking out schools was something else that had to be done, as most families with children move during the summer months so that there won't be any interruptions during the regular school year. My oldest daughter, Alex, had attended a rigorous high school in Houston that strictly focused on nurturing children who were interested in the medical profession. Although she was a 16 year old senior, she already had her certification in CPR and had worked as a student worker at the public hospital in the Medical District, Ben Taub. I figured her senior year would be completed at Archbishop Blenk High. My youngest daughter, Torey, was in the Duke University TIP program and was entering the 4th grade. Hynes Elementary was what I chose for her. After touring the schools and enrolling them both for the fall, I was beginning to feel right at home again; and so were they. We were all excited. And everyone was just as excited to see us back.

Besides the heat, getting revved up for the courses I needed to take to obtain my appraiser's license from the Real Estate Appraisers Board was pretty intense. I wanted to at least have 50% of the courses out of the way before the girls' school started in a couple of months. Even if I'm working or taking courses, everyone knows that I'm a hands on mom when it comes to my daughters' education. Every school that they've attended; every teacher and principal knew who Zelia was or 'Lisa' as I am so affectionately called. If I can help out after work or during my time off, they know they can always count on me to volunteer 110%. If you're wondering where the name 'Lisa' comes from;

anyone who's born and raised in New Orleans knows that your nickname oftentimes has nothing to do with your birth name. The youngest of six children, my older siblings wanted me to be named 'Lisa.' Momma and daddy, on the other hand, had other plans. So I was named after both grandmothers and when I came home from the hospital, my brothers and sisters called me 'Lisa.' That made sense, right? Only in New Orleans!

With school about to begin, I was one step closer to getting acclimated with what's considered the quality control standards of the Uniform Standards of Professional Appraisal Practice or USPAP. Between juggling my appraisal classes and getting the girls ready for school, my days were pretty much full.

As school for my daughters quickly approached, there were reports of a storm developing in the Gulf and its definite direction still had not been determined yet.

By now, I had completed my required classroom hours and passed the first half of courses taken in order to qualify, as required by law, to work side by side with the best. I had been diligently studying for what seemed to be two long hot months. And the intensity of the heat outside, felt like it was getting even hotter. It was Thursday, August 25, 2005, and the certificate that I held in my hand would be the last and only tangible document that I would receive, as I placed it in the trunk of my car, not knowing that what was about to take place in four days would fracture the Gulf Coast region and shock the entire nation.

THE EVACUATION

SATURDAY, AUGUST 27, 2005, I TOLD MY GIRLS TO START packing and to pack lightly this time, as the 11th hurricane of the season, Katrina, was intensifying in the Gulf of Mexico. Just a few weeks earlier, we had evacuated to a hotel downtown near Canal Street for a previous storm. This storm didn't pose a threat at all. No heavy rain or wind damage…just a trickle of rain. That's how it is when you live in a city that has hurricanes every year. Growing up with the realization of damaging storms, you knew that if the storm curved towards the east, you take the route going west… if it curved towards the west, then it was the east route. Houston, Atlanta, and Mississippi were normally our planned evacuation routes in the event that there was a category higher than a two. If we did have to take cover, we always looked at it as a mini vacation, as we always planned to stay no more than 3 or 4 days. We had more Vienna sausages, Spam, and crackers and cookies than we could ever ask for!

You see, the night before, my brother Glenn called me to tell me to put the t.v. on The Weather Channel. He said that he had just gotten a phone call from a friend who worked on the oil rigs in the Gulf of Mexico who told him that they were told to evacuate the rigs immediately because Hurricane Katrina was going to be pretty bad. He went on to say that the men who worked on those rigs hadn't evacuated from the previous storms. 2005 had gone on record to be the year with the most hurricane activity recorded in history. As the girls slept, we stayed on the phone and talked a minute while watching The Weather Channel together. *"Look at how big that storm is."* He then pointed out, *"I've never seen a storm that wide."* He was right. I had never seen one cover that much ground either. Still, no one appeared to be worried and talks on the news channels about the storm were not that great yet. Glenn said he was going to call daddy to let him know what the men on the oil rigs were instructed to do. *"I'm going to fax him this memo that went out."*

When we both hung up, I continued to watch t.v. changing channels from time to time to view other networks to see what comparisons, if any, were being made regarding the storm's progress. I decided to call Juan. We talked until the sun came up.

Not getting any sleep, Saturday morning came before you knew it. Most local channels were geared up talking about the arrival of Katrina. At this point, all evacuations were strictly voluntary. Before it was categorized as a hurricane, the storm moved through the Bahamas this past Wednesday and Thursday. It wasn't until it turned westward toward southern Florida and reached winds of 75 mph making it a Category 1 which classified it as a hurricane. It became Hurricane Katrina just before making landfall near Miami-Dade two days before we evacuated. It wasn't until it moved southwestward across southern Florida that it began to intensify.

I went to the gas station on Franklin Avenue to fill up my car and chatted a while with my close friend Tiger who is also the owner of the station. Lines were not long yet, as it was still pretty early in the morning. I didn't have to "make" any groceries because canned goods and perishables had already been stored from previous false alarmed hurricanes. In New Orleans, we say *"make groceries"* because it is the French way to say *'going to the grocery store'* and translated into English it means "to make groceries." That's just another Naturally N'awlins thing about this well loved city. We know you really can't make groceries. After giving Tiger a hug goodbye, I went back home to check on the girls and their progress with packing. *"Don't bring every outfit in your closet,"* I told them nicely. Last time, we brought a little too much and it was a false alarm. Although meteorologists began making comparisons of Hurricane Katrina to Hurricane Betsy of 1965, I couldn't really relate to those associations since I wasn't quite a year old when Hurricane Betsy hit. I had read about it and heard stories from my family members, but I couldn't get a full appreciation of the assessments.

While going from basically no talk at all about Hurricane Katrina from the meteorologists and local officials to comparing it to Hurricane Betsy overnight; during the previous storm, Alex and Torey brought their childhood and baby photo albums, along with many other unnecessary items. For this particular trip; however, I asked them to leave it at home. *"Since we have to leave ours this time, you have to leave yours too,"* they schemed. You see, I had a pretty big album that was still in the trunk of my car from our last false trip. Mine had pictures of me when I was a baby, sorority pictures, the girls…pretty much everything that had any significant meaning to me. *"Okay, deal."* I told them.

Although we were minimizing our luggage, I still allowed the girls to bring something special. Alex brought her pink blanket and her T-shirt that her dad and I gave her when I gave birth to Torey when she was 8 years old that had her picture airbrushed on the back with wording on the front that said, "I'm a Big Sister." Torey brought a game and her favorite purse. All three of us only took three articles of clothing since we figured we'd only be gone for three days. Torey just made nine years old, and wanted to bring her electric guitar and amplifier that she received from me at her birthday party a month ago, but it would have taken up too much space. Besides, we would be back home in three days anyway, or Wednesday at the latest.

After begging my dad to come with us; by noon, my mom, older sister Debra, niece Sheri, and my daughters and I were all headed to Houston, Texas without him. We cancelled the reservations in Georgia since the storm was expected to take a turn towards the east once it hit land. *"I'll go to the Superdome if it gets too bad. I'm used to riding out these storms you know,"* daddy assured us. Daddy, retired Lieutenant Ellis Williams, was a well respected Commander for the New Orleans Police Department. And was probably one of the smartest police officers on the force (Black or White). Many police officers admired and looked up to my dad. Then, of course, there were a few who couldn't believe that an African-American could be so smart. He's also an Associate Minister of Historic Second Baptist Church. He's had both these titles ever since I was born. Daddy came from a different generation...the frugal generation; where no matter how much money you made, you saved for a rainy day. He was intelligent, trustworthy, temperate demeanor, honest, brave, a sharp dresser when he had to be, handsome, tall, great teacher, a great provider, and a man of his word. A graduate and alumnus from Loyola University, daddy received three degrees, and is the author of two books. He looked like Bill Cosby. When any one of us had homework that we couldn't understand or that the teachers at school were unable to deliver, he was somehow able to teach us to understand any verbiage that we would read... and a wiz at math too! Daddy also had a way with words and sayings. *"There's more than one way to skin a cat,"* he'd always say. I think we all heard and recognized that one. You may have not understood them at the time it was said, but one day you could be making groceries or driving along Canal Street and then it would click. One of daddy's sayings was, *"People will always remember you if you're extremely smart or grossly dumb. People will also remember you if you're beautiful or ugly. People never remember you when you're average or in-between."* So remember this saying 'cause it will make sense later on. I am the only sibling that calls my dad "daddy" while my other brothers and sisters call our dad "Da-Da."

SUNDAY, AUGUST 28, 2005 – *"This is the big one ya'll,"* Mayor Ray Nagin said. Hurricane Katrina had become a Category 5 reaching significant strength with winds at 175 mph. Max Mayfield, National Hurricane Center Director, warned about the possible breaching of the levees and the potential for large loss of lives. As mandatory evacuations were underway, we had already settled in at our hotel in Houston's medical district. Since I had just moved from Houston two months ago, I took everyone out around town to visit with some of my friends. They were happy to see me, back so soon in Houston, and to meet some of my family members they had never seen before.

We called back home to check on our friends and family who decided to stay and ride out the storm. It wasn't out of the ordinary for people to stay. If you lived in certain areas of town, it was common for people to stay even in the worst of storms. Certain areas never flooded, and people's decision for staying was based on their comparison to Hurricane Betsy and the severity of the storm in their particular neighborhood. The rule was, if your neighborhood survived during Betsy, you stayed. Sometimes, a hurricane threat to the city was a chance to allow others to leave for a mini vacation.

We heard that the traffic was tied up on the interstate with people going west. Glenn and his family headed to Dallas. My brother Lathan, and his family headed to Houston too. Eventually, the direction to evacuate the city was routed to the east because there were too many people on the freeways headed west. Because of this, contra-flow was then directed for drivers to head eastward. Contra-flow is when all lanes coming into the city on the interstate are reversed and directed out of the city to aid in an emergency evacuation. So no one can come in and everyone can get out. Traffic on I-10 West in New Orleans looked like I-45 North in Houston looks on a daily basis. It seemed like the entire city was leaving! My sister Rita headed to Jackson, Tennessee as her older daughter Monique drove. Finally, they were routed eastward as well.

MONDAY, AUGUST 29, 2005 – Hurricane Katrina hit the Big Easy at approximately 9:45 a.m. CST. Storm surge flooding was 10-20 feet above normal tide levels along the southeastern Louisiana coast. Mayor Ray Nagin declared a State of Emergency, as mandatory evacuations were already underway. About 70% of the city is below sea level, and is protected by many levees. The highest levees are probably about 18 feet. It was predicted that the storm surge for the New Orleans area would reach about 18 feet. It was estimated that the nearly 20,000-25,000 people who remained had gone to the Louisiana Superdome for shelter. Many news stations were destroyed, and power and communications lost. *"This is a threat that we've never faced before,"* Nagin said. *"If we galvanize and gather around each other, I'm sure we will get through this."* Even the president at that time, George Bush, issued disaster declarations for Louisiana, Mississippi, and parts of southern Florida. *"We'll do everything in our power to help the people and communities affected by this storm,"* Bush said.

While listening to the weather stations and talking to friends back home after the worse part of the hurricane passed, I was told that some of the homes had wind damage and that there was no flood damage.

Later on that morning, *"I've gotten reports this morning that there is already water coming over some of the levee systems. In the lower ninth ward, we've had one of our pumping stations to stop operating, so we will have significant flooding, it is just a matter of how much,"* the Mayor said on the NBC Today Show. Then FEMA Director, Michael Brown, also warned Bush of the levees breaching and the possibility of a *"catastrophe within a catastrophe"* with people using the Superdome as a place to take shelter from the Hurricane.

Bush visited an Arizona resort to promote a Medicare Drug benefit. Later that evening, Bush traveled to California to promote the same Medicare Drug benefit. That night, then

Governor Kathleen Blanco requested assistance from Bush. However, being the caring person that he is, according to news reports, Bush went to sleep without honoring that request. It would be the most powerful storm to threaten the Gulf Coast region in decades.

TUESDAY, AUGUST 30, 2005 – The following morning, according to news reports, Bush gave a speech at the Naval base in Coronado, California. Around midday, Michael Chertoff, U.S. Secretary of Homeland Security, claimed to have just been alerted about the levees breaching. A Pentagon spokesman claimed that there were enough National Guard Troops in the region. Looting in the streets and at grocery and department stores became uncontrollable and would soon reach epidemic proportions. It was unbearably hot. People were losing confidence in the Mayor, the police, and the president. *"We're using exhausted, scarce police to control looting when they should be used for search and rescue while we still have people on rooftops,"* then Councilwoman Jackie Clarkson said. We would learn later that the U.S.S. Bataan, an 844-foot ship with hospital facilities, six operating rooms and beds for over 600 patients, sat nearby in the Gulf of Mexico empty and waiting for orders to help out with matters in New Orleans. That afternoon; however, Bush had another more important photo opp with Country singer Mark Willis. Later on that night, according to news reports, Bush returned to his Crawford ranch for a final night of vacation and slept in his comfortable bed.

504

EVERY FLOOR IN THE ENTIRE HOTEL WAS QUIET. We couldn't believe our eyes and what was happening in our beloved city. We were all dumbfounded and speechless. We all wondered if the flooding was only happening in certain parts of the city or every area. Reports were sketchy and all we kept getting when we tried to place calls to *anyone* back home in New Orleans was a busy signal.

In the midst of all of this, photos surfaced of Bush taking pictures with Senator John McCain celebrating McCain's birthday. FEMA Director, "Brownie," was placing requests to the wrong agencies for help. If that wasn't enough, according to news reports, Condoleezza "Condi" Rice, then Secretary of State, took in a Broadway Show. A day later, she was pictured buying several shoes worth thousands of dollars at the Ferragamo on 5th Avenue. With caring people like them, who needed enemies?

By Wednesday, the Los Angeles Times reported that tens of thousands of people were trapped in the Superdome and the conditions were worsening, as people were reportedly being raped, sleeping in urine, and all sanitary facilities were inoperable. People were dying. Bush took another photo opp flying over the City of New Orleans in turmoil in Air Force One, viewing wiped out bridges, slabs where houses once stood, and of course, the thousands of human beings who hadn't had any food to eat, cold or fresh water to drink, clean facilities to use, or a bath in days…in what was remembered as record hot temperatures.

I thought about my friends who stayed; the loved ones who thought that they would be okay because they lived in a sturdy home in areas where it never flooded. I wondered how they were doing, and if they had to go to the Superdome to take cover like the rest who had stayed behind. When we did reach someone, we had to talk quickly, as the phone would soon be disconnected. Once again, we were unable to communicate with anyone. CNN became our everyday focus and would soon be our daily station, as this would be the only way, for days to come, to get any sense of what was happening in New Orleans. Anyone placing a call to area code '504' was not going to get through. Anyone trying to make a call from that area code wasn't going to get through either, for that matter. All circuits were busy and most forms of communication were down. Trying to reach *anyone* during and after Hurricane Katrina was impossible.

Thank God my daddy left!! He went with my sister Rita and my niece Monique.

DEUX
MISSION IMPOSSIBLE

AFTER GETTING BUSY SIGNALS FOR HOURS, SOME brilliant young kid said, *"text them!"* So we did. Everyone young and old—every finger was texting like we've never texted before. I texted daddy first, but didn't get a response back. My daddy and Rita should have gotten settled in at the hotel already. I texted her and Monique too! After a few seconds, Monique texted me back. *"Do you see what's happening in New Orleans?!"* she texted. *"Yeah, I can't believe it!"* I said fearfully. We all wanted so desperately to know what was going on in our *own* neighborhoods. We wanted to know if our homes were safe, and if not, just how much water got in them. *"Tell daddy to check his cell phone. We've been trying to get in touch with him for the longest!"* I said. *"I will, I don't think he knows how to check his text messages. I'll show him how,"* Monique responded. *"We're all doing fine."* my dad finally texted. *"How is everybody doing where you are?"* I was glad to hear that they were doing fine. A sigh of relief, I knew then that all of my family members were all safe and protected. I also knew then that it would take the older people a minute to get used to the texting. Too bad my dad, sister and niece were in Tennessee and we were in Texas.

I tried to reach my friends back home to see if they had made it out of the city and if they were okay. Lynell and her husband were trapped on the second floor of their home. *"We have food and water that we brought upstairs a couple of days ago."* she texted. They were able to reach the fire department and were waiting for the search and rescue team to come and get them. She said, *"With all the water surrounding the houses, it is difficult for the police and fire departments to figure out exactly where we are."* Watching the news, it was even difficult for *us* to figure out what neighborhoods the media were in too. Everything and every neighborhood we saw were unrecognizable.

I've known Lynell and her husband Bobby for 11 years now. The greatest couple you ever want to meet. Lynell and I have one thing in common…okay two—children and food. And, not necessarily in that order. Anything that has to do with youth and it's positive; we're both involved in it. I met Lynell when Alex was in the sixth grade at Jean Gordon Elementary. She replaced Alex's teacher in the middle of the school year. What a wonderful replacement. Lynell was awesome! She fit right in. She's knowledgeable, crafty, funny, and could get those kids "wowed" up about coming to school. We *all* loved her. Lynell could throw down too. She could cook up a meal anytime. If you were to ever stop over at Lynell's house, you'd be in for a really good treat. I don't know who cooks the best—Lynell or Bobby. It didn't matter though. Whatever was on the menu was always good.

I tried to reach another good friend of mine, Pam, and wasn't able to reach her immediately either. When I did get her, she told me that she and her family were in Richmond, Texas with her sister.

Pam is like a sister to me. We have tons of stuff in common. Pam's beautiful, smart, great at decorating, friendly, an entrepreneur, and down to earth. Making Shrimp or Crawfish Etouffee or any type of Creole cuisine was Pam up and down. Her family used to own a restaurant. I met Pam 18 years ago at Jean Gordon too, when Alex was in Kindergarten. You see, Pam hurt her finger one day and Alex told me about it when she came home from school. The very next day, Alex ran up to "Ms. Pam" and asked how her finger was doing. Pam told me that although her finger incident was a minor one, that not one teacher or student had inquired about how she was doing the next day... except for my daughter, Alexiz. Pam went on to say how thoughtful and compassionate Alex was. I already knew that though. At only four, I had already known that Alex was a unique and concerned child. I was really glad that Pam was okay.

I then put in a call to Edgar. Even though some people had evacuated out of the city, I was beginning to realize that no matter where these people were, if their area code was '504,' the circuits were busy. Edgar and his family had evacuated to Garland, Texas. *"We're all doing fine,"* he texted. Mr. Beady Bead, as I jokingly call him, was all right.

I first met Edgar 20 years ago, when I became the Adviser for the Mayor's housing office. I started off as a temp with the City of New Orleans and after only two weeks of working, I was told that all the temporary employees would be laid off. Just my luck! Just started working for two weeks, get one check, and laid off already! The City was trying to find a way to lower the budget. Getting rid of the 187 temps was the answer. I had worked so diligently those two weeks, taking on more assignments and tasks than what they had originally asked me to do. I even developed a brochure for the Bureau of Revenue department so that new and tenured business owners could place their comments regarding their transactions with the City and the type of service that was delivered, and to tell us how we could make their experiences better. In the end, they decided to keep only three temps and make them permanent employees. To my surprise, I, along with two men, were the chosen ones. After only two weeks, I was the only female who was kept on, and the other temps who had been there for nine months were let go. Imagine that!

After becoming a permanent employee, I was then transferred from the Bureau of Revenue to the Mayor's Division of Housing and Neighborhood Development where I would eventually become the liaison to the Mayor's office and Congressional offices, and monitor for multiple HUD housing programs. That is where I met Edgar. I was one of the few who had access to the IDIS system for you savvy federal grants management people. Well, one day, I overheard Edgar, who I didn't know at the time, talking about me to other office staff as they were all wondering if my hair was a wig or a weave. Those were the only two choices, as if it couldn't be my own, right?! Word on the street was that it was a wig. Edgar's vote; however, was a weave. Back then, weaves were not as common as they are today. Wigs weren't either. Well, I had walked up on them… talking about my hair, because it *was* my own hair. Of course everyone denied that there was a bet. So ever since then, Edgar gave me the nickname of "Ms. Weave." To get back at Edgar, I started calling him 'Beady Bead.' You remember that Martin Show where Martin Lawrence plays himself, and on this one episode he calls Pam, Gina's best friend, 'Beady Bead' because he said she had *beads* in the back of her hair? Well, for the record, Edgar doesn't really have beads in the back of his head. I don't think so anyway. That was just my way of getting back at him for making people think I had a weave. I guess after calling him Mr. Beady Bead for so long, well, I guess it sorta stuck. Mr. Beady

Bead and his family were out of harm's way. You know, all of my close friends are jewels. I value everything about them. They are truly one of a kind.

I then tried to get in touch with Mr. Howard. Not only a good friend with great words of wisdom; Mr. Howard was also my best neighbor. If you lived near the Lakefront, there wasn't anyone who didn't know him. He was like another grandfather to my daughters. I guess as you get older and as you experience 'life' people can come up with all sorts of sayings. Mr. Howard often told my girls the same thing that my mom and dad would tell them. *"Get an education and never let anything get in your way."* Mr. Howard would also say, *"Make sure that your circle of friends know more than you."* Alex could never figure that saying out when she was a little girl. And that particular saying would bother her the most. She couldn't figure out for the life of her why Mr. Howard would want one of her friends to be 'smarter' than her. You see, it wasn't that Mr. Howard wanted someone to be smarter than Alex. He knew how smart she was and simply wanted her and Torey to be around others who were just like them. His thought was that you couldn't learn from someone who was less intelligent. Mr. Howard was a widower and one of the nicest people you'd ever want to meet. He had one son. His home phone was down like everyone else's and I didn't know his son's cell phone number to see how they were doing. He enjoyed leisurely walks in the neighborhood stopping along the way and talking to everyone he could. If you were outside in the garden, he'd lend a hand to help out. If you were on your patio eating lunch or dinner, he'd come over for a bite to eat too. He was welcomed by everyone in the community. The only time you didn't see Mr. Howard strolling along the avenue was between 6:30-7:00 p.m. That was because Wheel of Fortune was on. Most people in New Orleans watch Wheel of Fortune. Even if you weren't watching it, it was tuned in on that channel playing in the background.

Mr. Howard looked like the character Ed Norton from The Honeymooners. I met him when I first moved into our neighborhood on the Lakefront.

I remember coming home from work one day and a tree stump that was on the side of our home was cut all the way down. We had a corner lot on St. Roch and Vienna. St. Roch Avenue—naturally 'Nawlins, right? My then husband had cut it down but couldnât (or wouldn't) cut it all the way down to the ground. It was an eye sore. I guess Mr. Howard felt the same way. Well, when I came home from work one day, it was completely gone. I assumed my husband did it and really didn't pay any more attention to it, until my husband came home from work and asked me if I got someone to remove thc stump. I told him I didn't and that I thought *he* did it. Of course, I should have known he didn't. Like Dr. Phil says, "What was *I* thinking?" Well, the very next day, Saturday, someone rang our doorbell and who else other than, Mr. Howard. This would be our first meeting and many, many more meetings to come. He began to introduce himself and asked us if we liked the "missing" tree stump. We all laughed and told him that we loved it. We thanked him and asked him how much did we owe him. To our surprise, Mr. Howard said proudly, *"Nothing, I did it myself."* Well, well, well. I thought. You see, my husband was tall and athletic. I knew I liked that neighborhood already. Only time would tell if Mr. Howard and his son were okay.

Watching the news became an everyday occurrence. We tuned in diligently and desperately to see if national news channels would show the different neighborhoods in the city in hopes that we would see our homes and assess the damages, if any. We waited anxiously to see the zip codes and areas that were shown since we were just unsure as to what our futures held. It was going on the second week and getting a hold to someone locally was a complete waste of time. Placing calls to some of the policemen we knew was a lost cause too. It was nearly impossible to reach anyone.

COMPUTER 101

BY NOW, WE WERE GOING INTO OUR THIRD WEEK AND realizing that we were not going to be able to go back home as quickly as we'd thought. The news stories were all starting to sound the same–hopeless. After being completely numb and watching the City saturated in water for weeks, there was no sign of life in most of the neighborhoods. I had hoped for the best and was grateful that my family was okay.

Every household was instructed to apply for federal assistance with the Federal Emergency Management Agency (FEMA) or what they would soon earn the affectionate title of locally as the Federal Emergency Managing Assholes (FEMA). Whether you wanted them to be or not, FEMA became a household name and what would soon be one of many agencies full of inefficiencies, gross mismanagement, and widespread corruption.

Doing business with FEMA was no easy task, and you had better known how to use a computer or wait on the phone for hours for some of the most unpleasant people you ever want to speak with. When you did get someone who seemed to be caring and inoffensive, you just wanted to reach through the phone and hug them. Most hotels these days may have a couple of computers in the lobby for courtesy purposes. I'm sure that no one ever expected that 60% of hotel residents would be in need for a computer at the rate that we needed them during the aftermath of Hurricane Katrina. Luckily, I knew my way around Houston. So I'd go to the Bellaire library which was near my home when I lived there. What about those who were not familiar with this city or any other city that people evacuated to? You could also sign up and register on FEMA's toll free number if you didn't have access to a computer. With thousands of people calling federal and state agencies for assistance in record numbers, everyone was stunned at what was happening to them, and uncertain as to what lay ahead. Providing a picture ID and being drilled about your identity became a daily task.

No one had copies of their birth certificates, social security cards, recent bank statements, mortgage statements, or insurance papers. Hell, five years later, I still don't have my official birth certificate. With all the road barriers you had to go through just to prove your identity, it became more repulsive than just a simple act of duty...even with companies you had done business with for years. *"Ohh, uhh-uhh!" It was a nightmare!"* And with only three days of clothing packed, going on four weeks—well, you can imagine.

Everyone was passed the flabbergasted stage. We were at the "I can't believe this is happening" stage. "Why was this happening to us...our city?" Some critics seemed to think that this was somehow our fault and that New Orleans was destined to go down because of homosexuals living in the city and something to do with the French Quarter. When I heard this, I quickly realized that we live a "C" average country, and immediately understood how George Bush could be president.

Everywhere we went for assistance, whether it was to file a claim with the insurance company or to get money out of the bank, we were watched with a careful eye. Thanks to the events that led up to the Superdome saga, we were all classified as complete hoodlums, we were all considered as ignorant, and we were now called "refugees." *Ohh uhh-uhh! Refugees!* Yep. We had a president whose IQ appeared to be lower than a "C-".

After realizing that we were here indefinitely, I knew I had to get the girls back in their schools and get a job. I told Juan that the girls and I would be living back in Houston indefinitely.

As usual, schools in Houston had already started—going on five weeks to be exact. I visited the principal at Torey's old school in Meyerland where previously she was an honors student and was able to get her enrolled in the fourth grade. Because Alex was an entering senior, this would have been her last year at her old high school. Her school; however, had a very rigorous curriculum and if you missed five weeks, you missed an awful lot. Her freshman year started off with over 400 students. By this time, her senior year, there was only a little over 100 left. Remember, this school focused on getting children ready for the medical field. It was imperative that every student kept up.

Fearing that Alex had already missed too many days her senior year, I was unable to get her re-enrolled back at her old familiar high school. The Assistant Administrator placed a call in to a fairly new high school that Bill and Melinda Gates funded which focused on children graduating with an Associate's Degree. Alex already had her state required high school credits and only needed English IV to graduate. We visited the school, enrolled her in the class she needed and was also told that she qualified for college courses at the university next door. Moving back to New Orleans two months before Hurricane Katrina and then moving back to Houston unexpectedly was a challenge for Alex. She took it extremely hard for the remainder of the year.

She was always used to a stable home environment. Living out of a hotel was exciting for Torey, as "The *Suite* Life of Zack and Cody" was one of her favorite Disney sitcom's at the time. Alex, on the other hand, was ready to go home. And so was I.

SCATTERED

IT WAS REPORTED THAT EVACUEES WERE SPREAD throughout 49 states across the country. Imagine that! Most were in Houston and Atlanta. For many, this evacuation would be the first time, not that they had evacuated, but the first time that they had lived anywhere else besides New Orleans.

New Orleans was unique like that. It had its own special qualities. People from all over the world would come to visit the city year round. It was a well known tourist attraction. Known for its historical buildings, fabulous French and Creole cuisine, 'naturally' beautiful down to earth people, and the French Quarter, my hometown was one of the most traveled to cities in America. Something sinister, though, was taking place. In addition to the nonchalant attitude of the Chief of Staff, the military were separating families, mothers from their babies, and fathers from their wives and children spreading them all over the United States. Families were purposely separated en masses. Nothing was being done to prevent or stop this type of exodus from happening. Watching scenes like this play out on national television was heart-breaking. There was widespread pandemonium. Evacuation initiatives for the remaining residents in the city were completely senseless. No thought or preparation was put into the departure of tens of thousands of what appeared to be a vast majority of African-American people. It was compassionless, malicious, and utterly reckless.

While people back home were being routed to just about everywhere, my family and I were in Houston, Dallas, and Tennessee going through a bitter battle ourselves. Having to provide information that you didn't have within your possession, at times, posed somewhat of a challenge. I began to hate that I ever moved back to New Orleans. Just when you think you've planned everything out, life throws you a curve ball.

I knew I had better start getting my personal affairs in order so I contacted my mortgage-company, and insurance provider to fill out the paperwork to file a claim. For the first time, I was conducting business "outside" in 100° plus temperatures on the west side of Houston under a tent. In the past decade since I have had insurance, I NEVER had to meet the home owner's insurance agents outside. NEVER! I thought, "This is downright ridiculous!" Police were on hand and long lines existed in a grocery store parking lot.

An agent who was sitting down stood up and walked over to me to ask if I was there to file a claim due to Hurricane

Katrina. *"Yes, I am,"* I said discouragingly. *"Is that your vehicle?"* the agent asked with a puzzled look on his face. *"Yes it is."* I responded. *"The Mercedes...that's yours?* He asked again! *"Yeah, why? Am I parked illegally?!"* I replied. "So that's your Mercedes?" He went on to ask again as he came closer to where I was standing in line. Out of dozens of people in line, in that scorching sun, I began to wonder why I was getting all of the unwelcomed attention. I felt like I had pulled up in the wrong vehicle. *"Ohh, uhh-uhh, You know, it is HOT out here and I've never had to make a payment to my insurance agent outside or conduct professional business Outside?! I know this storm was pretty big, but you guys know you could have come up with a better way to treat your <u>loyal</u> customers? What's up with this?"* I said as I was getting pissed off. *"We wanted to make sure that we are able to assist everyone as quickly as possible."* He said. What the heck was that all about? I guess he decided to back down after *me* asking *him* questions. Did he think that people from New Orlenas don't have cars like mine?! Why is everybody judging us? It's a good thing momma wasn't here. He definitely would have been told something from "Ma Dear." Just like my brothers and sisters call our dad "Da-Da" they call our mom "Ma Dear." And believe me; if you have a Ma Dear in your family, you know exactly what I'm talking about. Momma didn't play.

Momma is *beautiful* like Lena Horne but quick-witted like Della Reese. Momma was fast to put someone in their place...man or woman. Her motto was, *"If they can dish it, they can take it."* She taught me just about everything. As a child, I loved to cook with her. Momma cooked everything from scratch. No boxed cakes, Jiffy cornbread, or Blue Runner Red Beans at our house. She had a voice like an angel. She sang like an opera singer with a strong Alto voice, and played the piano and guitar. She was selfless. She's just naturally beautiful and talented. And she read some of the greatest bedtime stories where every character in the story line had their own unique voice. With her, I learned how to sew and made my very first skirt when I was in the 4th grade. She even taught me how to whistle. My girls to this day are still intrigued at how loud I sound and tease me about sounding exactly like or better than what I am trying to imitate.

Daddy worked day and night so that he could provide for all eight of us. Therefore, momma was the disciplinarian in his absence. Now momma was bad enough, but if daddy had to discipline you when he came home, you could hang it up. She would say cuss words that hadn't even been invented yet. And my three brothers were always into something; whether it was at home or at Carver Senior High where they attended school. If the cussing didn't do it, there was always that baseball bat, machete, and knife on hand at her disposal. That was momma's trinity. She had her trinity in the kitchen (onions, celery, and bell pepper), and her trinity for protection. That knife was pretty dull though. I always wondered what she thought she could possibly do with a dull knife. I guess the thought of her and her arsenal of weapons was visually frightening enough for us.

Then there was always that one sibling who always took it to the next level. Cutting class and getting in trouble, my oldest brother died when I was in the 10th grade. I was the only child who never got whipped by momma or daddy. You know why? I was the *smartest* one. After seeing momma's trinity and the wrath of daddy when my other five brothers and sisters did something wrong, I knew I had better do just the opposite to stay clean. All my life, I did just that.

Daddy would always tell momma that she had expensive taste. Thank God she did. I always told daddy that he dressed like a box of Crayolas...donned in every color all at the same time. Remember daddy was only G-Q when he had to be, and then it was momma who would always fix him up. Momma dressed like Ms. Chancelor from the "Young and the Restless." Whether she had to go out somewhere or was simply staying inside at home with us, _all_ year round she was always dolled up. Momma was definitely the ultimate "Superwoman" before Karen White was.

Enduring long lines in the heat of the day to repair your life and get everything back on track was the order of business each day. Hitting the insurance lines for your homeowner's coverage, talking on the cell phone because you didn't have a home phone anymore to conduct business and waiting for hours or sometimes weeks to get connected to the appropriate person who's handling your claim was tiring. Oftentimes, it could be humiliating speaking with people on the other end of the phone that already had a preconceived notion as to the type of individual or person they thought you were. All of this while paying hundreds of dollars to your cell phone company for calls made to conduct business. Thank God my cell phone provider allowed their customers to make calls free of charge if the call was to a toll free number. This way, I could ask the company I needed to conduct business with if they had a toll free number to call them back.

While I attempted to get my life back on track, my daughters were also dealing with school work and trying to get used to living in a hotel which quickly became unexciting. Daily, my entire family was going in different directions while we all endured long exhausting lines.

My friend who lived in Ohio, Adrienne, mailed a box of clothes for me and the girls. Adrienne and I first met our freshman year in college. She was in my wedding and I in hers. She and George have two beautiful girls. She's also originally from Louisiana. We've been friends for quite some time now.

Daddy was finally able to get a flight from Tennessee to Houston so that he could be with momma. In their 70's, they too, were trying to get their lives back on track.

I came from a stable home environment. I grew up in a four-bedroom home in the upper 9th Ward that was later converted to a three-bedroom so that momma could have a dining room. In the 5th grade, I got a piano for Christmas and started taking lessons. I lived at the same address until I got married. My children were also used to stability. Katrina had interrupted everything and placed the goals and dreams of thousands on hold.

Meanwhile, my girlfriends in Houston would take turns inviting me and my family over for dinner and home cooked meals. While visiting Vera for dinner one day, we learned that she was going through some personal challenges herself having medical tests done. I met Vera when I first moved to Houston in 2001. She's originally from Louisiana too. Vera had a heart that was big as gold. We would stay hours on the phone talking about everything! She too, gave great advice. She was like a big sister to me when I lived in Houston before I moved back to New Orleans. Going over to her house felt like home, and the food was just like home too.

One Sunday, Anna and Bruce had a *huge* dinner at their home for us. Actually, we pigged out on fried catfish, fried shrimp, French fries, hushpuppies, salad, dessert, the whole works!! Alex used to date Anna's son. They gave us boxes of clothes and their hospitality was very much welcomed. They've always been and still are an *amazing* couple. Houston had opened its arms to all the evacuees from Hurricane Katrina and the welcome was unbelievably enormous. I don't know of any other city that opened their arms and welcomed New Orleanians like the City of Houston did. We were feeling pretty much okay, as well to be expected after losing every personal possession… and for some…their loved ones.

FOOD STAMPS (PART I)

WHEN THE NEWS MEDIA ANNOUNCED THAT HURRICANE KATRINA evacuees could obtain food stamps for one month, everybody was at the food stamp office. They shut certain offices down for a few days so that they could cater to the large number of evacuees. We weren't tardy for that party. When we got there, the line was wrapped around the building...a couple of times. You would've thought that they were giving away a couple of houses or something. They *certainly* were giving something good. And *I* was definitely interested.

When we stepped inside, it was standing room only. Truth be told, looking back, this was probably the only agency that was organized and efficient. When I say everyone who could be there was there...they were. There were doctors, lawyers, teachers, nurses, every profession was there seeking help. And *everybody* was orderly, quiet, and speechless. I believe we were all in complete shock! We were all somehow trying to justify the fact that we were getting this type of assistance by knowing that we've contributed to the system and somehow knowing that, well, now it was our turn. All you needed was your Louisiana driver's license and picture ID. What about me? I just moved back home two months before Hurricane Katrina! I still had my Texas driver's license! What about me?! Thank God I wasn't turned away. They required all of us to give our fingerprints to get the assistance. STEAKS FOR EVERYONE!!! Well, at least for one month anyway.

I then went to the Social Security office to get a duplicate social security card for me and the girls. I did all of this while they were at school. Each day we would get up, get them ready for school, drop them off and I would begin my day going to the different agencies in an attempt to regain my identity. Giving your fingerprint for basic services for Katrina victims became a way of life. I'd love to know if this was a standard for all groups of races.

Now the Social Security office was a different kind of agency. They market themselves as being one of the "best places to work." Their process, however, was somewhat antiquated. When I attempted to get my daughter's cards, I was told that my children's names could not be hyphenated even though their original Social Security card had their names with a hyphen. My daughters do not have middle names, and their first names are hyphenated. Why couldn't this office hyphenate the name that they had been given at birth? The reason was that there wasn't a "hyphen" on the computer! Trying not to do a 'Ma Dear,' I tried to patiently explain where the hyphen was located. So there I was feeling like I was giving my verbal dissertation. While the person that assisted me appeared to be intrigued at what I was saying and that there was a remote possibility of a "hyphen" existing, in complete exultation, this theory was then taken to the next level—the supervisor. I know I played Dorothy my freshman year in high school, but could I have possibly walked in to the land of 'Oz?!' With much excitement myself, I was finally going to see the man behind the curtain. The supervisor assured me that there was a hyphen on the computer but that after 1996, the agency could no longer place hyphens on anyone's social security card. How convenient considering that my youngest daughter was born in 1996. The explanation that was given to me sounded redunkulous! I can see it now. "Congressional order given to 'eliminate all hyphens' on social security cards."

So there I am on my cell phone calling the U.S. Social Security office in D.C. to report a hyphen-less computer and an instituted Congressional order to cease and desist with placing hyphens on all social security cards. Ohh, uhh-uhh! What a day! To keep from having to go back to the Social Security office at a later date, as I had already made several previous trips, I agreed to get the social security cards without the hyphens in their names. Desperately trying to get our identity back, my daughters' *new* social security cards read:

Alexizchloe Brown

Kaylantorey Brown

It made it look like I was drunk when I named them and just went crazy with the alphabets! Then it hit me, their schools from last year had all of their info (i.e.: medical records, birth certificates, and social security numbers). While we were all slowly *losing* our identity, I was rigorously getting things back in motion by applying for numerous jobs and reconnecting with the appraiser's office. When their new card arrived in the mail, it just didn't look right. Their names were not right at all! I had no other choice but to use the *copies* of their social security card that I received from their schools instead of the replacements.

My family and I checked out of the hotel and were invited to stay with Vera until we found a place to stay. Our zip codes were still not allowed back in to New Orleans. We were extremely home sick and curious to find out how our homes were fairing out. Thanksgiving had passed which was the first year EVER that the entire family did not celebrate together in New

Orleans at momma and daddy's. We still couldn't believe that this was happening. While others were quick to discriminate, Katrina, on the other hand, did not.

We moved back to New Orleans after the girls finished up their school year in Houston. My house had taken in 10 feet of water damage, a couple of holes in the roof, and a year's worth of mold. Rooms that used to be mauve and cream were no longer vibrant colors and all of a sudden were black, white, and gray. The new colors of New Orleans were symbolic to the disparaging relief efforts that residents received from the Road Home program. Hefty grant awards were given to some White residents while Black residents received 30% less. Procedures to execute the program had Gray areas. Still, one year later, some neighborhoods looked as if Hurricane Katrina had just happened!

We moved in with my sister, Debra, on the Westbank, as thousands of other residents moved to the Westbank due to all the damage to the homes on the Eastbank. Debra is a registered nurse. Momma and daddy stayed there too. Glenn, Lathan, and Rita had no place to stay. All of our homes were severely damaged and uninhabitable. All of our family pictures were gone. And because we all lost our homes, we could not call on each other for assistance. All of our clothing, furniture, collectibles—everything gone! My "Keys to the City" that I received in elementary for two consecutive years from Mayor

Moon Landrieu for academic accolades—gone. With that honor, I had been given a tour of the city in a helicopter…during a time when education meant something in this country and, particularly, in the Black community. And being the same size since high school, I lost over 20 years of clothing. My sorority pin—gone! My sister's sorority pin, as she gave it to me to hold for her—gone! Momma and daddy's savings bonds and all their other valuables that were locked up in a special place at their home—gone! They lost over $200,000 worth of furniture alone. Our family bible that daddy had before I was born, birth certificates—anything of importance, all of a sudden had quickly become just a memory. And you know they don't make anything like they used to anymore. I no longer had video tapes to pop in to watch of my children's birthday parties, school ceremonial activities, or them simply clowning around when they were little. My coin collection was completely gone! My girls' christening gowns and christening records were gone too. Their baby footprints and handprints that the hospital gave me when they were born—gone! All of their school-made Mother's Day gifts—gone! And the outfit they first wore when they came home from the hospital—gone! Their first baby picture—gone! Torey's brand new guitar and amplifier, and $400.00 that she got for her 9th birthday—all gone! All the pictures of me and Juan and the places we went, and the sentimental gifts he gave me… gone. Uptown, the Lakefront, and the 9th Ward—most of our homes were totally uninhabitable. Momma and daddy's home of over 40 years, the home we all grew up in at 3108 Metropolitan Street, would no longer be the home for the holidays. The shock began to set in all over again. Momma's 299 BIG church hats— gone! Well, at least she won't be blocking anybody's view at church anymore. My sister's home on the Westbank had damage too but at least it was livable.

I started working helping victims of Hurricane Katrina get assistance through the Clinton/Bush Katrina Fund, Operation HOPE, through its phenomenal director, Oliver.

One Saturday, to get out of the crowded house, the girls and I decided to go to our favorite spot, Café Du Monde, to get beignets, café au lait, and chocolate milk. Alex was now a freshman at Xavier University and Torey in the 5th grade at Trinity Episcopal. Most of the schools had not come back online yet. And the ones that were back did not deliver the same type of educational fortitude that was given in the past. As we left Jax Brewery and walked down Decatur to the Café, I noticed a woman continuously staring at me. She was walking with two other women and kept looking at me as if she knew me. As she stared with curiosity in her eyes, she finally walked over. *"Excuse me, I don't normally do this…but…there's something about your aura!"* this mysterious woman said. The two women she was with continued to walk as they were attempting to get in the long line to order their beignets. I concluded that she must have been a Palm Reader. The French Quarter is where many of the Palm Readers work. *"Could I read your palm, there's something you really need to know...I won't charge,"* she said frantically. *"No thanks,"* I said as I raised my left brow. Appearing to be discouraged, the Palm Reader walked away towards her friends who were waiting for her in line.

What was it that she wanted to say? What could she have possibly wanted to tell me about my future? Was it something good or was there something worse than Katrina about to happen? Heaven forbid! Out of all the years living in New Orleans, I had never had a fortune teller approach me. NEVER! That day stayed on my mind until I received an email the following month in October.

While I worked with Operation HOPE, I attempted again to get in touch with Jim Thorn's office. After several phone calls, I had finally made contact, spoken to, and gotten acceptance to work with one of the most revered, and sought after and respected Appraisers in the city; Jim Thorns of Jim Thorns Consulting. Jim is noted to be one of the most knowledgeable Appraisers in the city who has provided litigation support concerning Federal, State, District and Local courts. Anyone who has the privilege to work under his tutelage and leadership would surely gain a wealth of knowledge. Being the super lady that I am, not being able to wear dresses and high heels took some getting used to, as

I knew it wouldn't fit in with the day to day tasks of measuring residential homes and the "go hard or go home" approach of an appraiser. None-the-less, I hung in there, tennis shoes and all, to get the job done.

Previously, I had put in an application for employment with ICF and the Louisiana Road Home Program for a Compliance Specialist position; as I had an extensive background monitoring federally funded housing programs. While my friend Hank and I were out to lunch from Operation HOPE, I received a call on my cell phone from ICF asking if they could conduct a 30 minute phone interview. I politely told her yes, and placed her on hold to tell Hank that I would be a minute on the phone. I did the interview right in front of Hank, as it lasted approximately 40 minutes and was offered the job.

That same night, I received a phone call from the girl I went out with last September in Houston when I first met Juan. She asked me if we were still seeing each other. She said she had something to show me and if I was near a computer. I had just gotten off the phone with Juan earlier and the conversation with this girl was getting strange. I asked her what was this about and she told me to check my email because she was going to send me an email about Juan that someone had sent to her.

I pulled up my email account and opened the email that was just forwarded. The original email was dated seven months earlier than the October 9, 2006 date of when I received it. The original sender of the email had been erased. The email was about Juan and was sent from someone that knew him to several people including the girl that knew me. Knowing that the email would be hurtful and surprising to me, the girl who knew me forwarded the email so that I could know who the real Juan truly was.

At first, I thought the email was a sick joke. I couldn't believe what I was reading. Could this have been what the Fortune Teller was trying to tell me? I must have looked at the pictures in that email a dozen times before I called Debra and told her to come and see it. Debra even said the email couldn't be true. Was this possible?! She said the only way to find out for sure was to call Juan and tell him to go to his computer so that I could send it to him. I had been seeing Juan now for a little over two years. Momma and daddy adored him.

About 10 minutes after I forwarded him the email, Juan called. We stayed on the phone for the next 42 hours nonstop. *"You can't believe everything in that email Lisa. It's not what you think it is."* While Juan was not in the two pictures that were in the email that was forwarded to me, he spent hours trying to convince me that the email was not a reflection of who he was. Juan talked endless about how we were perfect together and how he never imagined meeting someone like me. He told me that he loved me, that the email wasn't true, and that I had to believe *him*. Juan flew in to New Orleans later on that week and stayed for six days to make sure that I knew he loved me…and the girls and that it's not him trying to hurt us. Everyone always thought that Juan and I were *great* together. So did I, until I got that email.

TROIS
REPORT TO ONE AMERICAN PLACE

ON MY WAY TO BATON ROUGE, WHILE PARKING MY CAR, I received a phone call Virginia. She chatted for a while and interjected and told me that because of my extensive knowledge, the company wanted me to start sooner than what Human Resources (HR) had originally told me. I told her that I was just on my way to sign all the paperwork and that I was in the parking garage. After signing all the paperwork in HR, I met Virginia, the Assistant Director of multi-family housing. *"I didn't expect you to look the way you look!"* she said shockingly. I ignored the awkward comment, as it was our first meeting since we spoke on the phone and said, *"It's a pleasure to meet you. I'm Zelia."* I quickly renegotiated the terms with her regarding me starting sooner.

Meanwhile, Virginia's friend Bill came into the office and introduced himself as the Director. Immediately after he said his name, he asked, *"Do you know how to write waivers?"* I replied, *"Yes I do, but what type of waivers are you thinking about writing when policy hasn't been written, according to Virginia?"* Virginia told him that she already spoke to me about starting sooner than the original planned date of January 2007.

In a previous discussion with HR, I was told that my office would be in New Orleans. I chose New Orleans since I was more familiar with the territory, housing structure, architecture, and overall community environment. With the new news of starting 90 days earlier and also working in Baton Rouge until my office was ready in New Orleans, I requested a vehicle and corporate lodging for the time that I would be stationed in Baton Rouge.

Afterwards, Virginia politely stood up, reached in her butt to pull out her draws, and nodded her head in agreement to the new terms as she extended her not-so-pristine "ass-digging hand" out to shake mine. "Ohh, uhh-uhh!" I thought. Thinking quickly, I immediately put my purse in my right hand and my briefcase in my left hand so that I wouldn't have to shake hers, and nodded my head and said, *"Looking forward to working with you...see you on Monday."* Virginia began to follow me out as she talked and walked with me towards my car.

At first impression, sitting across from Virginia as she sat behind her desk, she looked as if the airlines still had most of her luggage. But when she stood up to walk me out the door, I was even more surprised. Virginia donned eyeglasses, had light brown hair that was freshly messed up, and wore a brown shirt that was buttoned-up incorrectly—you know, where the first button isn't buttoned and the second button is placed through the first hole enclosure on the opposite side of a blouse. But that wasn't as bad as what I would eventually witness when she came from behind her desk. Virginia had on beige gaucho pants, you know the ones from the '70's, and these actually looked like she had them since then, and sported flip-flops on her un-pedicured feet!! Forgetting the flip-flops for a minute, I hadn't seen gaucho's since *I was* in elementary wearing them myself! What the hell?! I know I can be pretty chic-corporate with my arsenal of clothing; but Virginia didn't dress like most business women in charge or of authority.

I wore a Black Tahari suit, black and white pinstripe blouse with cufflinks, black Via Spiga closed toe shoes, and a pearl necklace.

As she walked and talked, she told me that she was brought on by her good friend Bill who was the first one hired in the program who called her to come down from the northwest coast where she resided to make some money since her background was in managing apartments. I would later learn that Virginia was also a fisherman in Alaska.

I began to find it odd that she walked me not only to the elevator, but out the door, down the street, and to my vehicle. I've been walked to the elevator before, but never to the car. Her behavior was not synonymous with that of a Director.

Who knew that later down the road that ICF and the Louisiana Road Home Program would eventually wound up being as questionable as the leadership that ran the program.

Virginia was the only person who saw the type of vehicle I drove.

As I drove back to New Orleans, I started having a Scooby Doo moment. I talked to my family members about my meeting with Virginia and also told Oliver that I had gotten the position. Oliver was sad to see me go but happy because he said, *"You can help out so many more people with your talent."* They all knew that I wanted to help out in every capacity. According to Virginia, I would be the third person hired for the Small Rental Property Repair program.

There were two components to the Road Home Program. The Housing Assistance Program (HAP) for single-family unit homeowners and the Small Rental Property Repair Program for multi-family unit landlords and homeowners. The HAP program had already opened up to the public and was making negative headlines daily. Much to the world's discovery later, the Small Rental Property Repair Program would be no different, coming under a barrage of inquisitions regarding unnecessary spending on the inside, and overall mismanagement of the entire program.

Managing apartments is great. But the program that I worked in wasn't about managing apartments. It was about monitoring a federally funded program and being familiar with the Code of Federal Regulations. Having a grants management background along with federally funded program management experience should have been a priority in the skill sets selected in order to run a program of this magnitude. From the way they physically appeared to their lack of monitoring federally funded programs, not ONE of my questions could be answered regarding the overall goals and implementation of the program.

It was October of 2006, and we were scheduled to open our doors to the public in spring of next year, almost two years after a major catastrophe. The citizens were counting on us.

The last weekend in October, my family and I celebrated my dad's surprise 75th birthday at Cannon's Restaurant on St. Charles Avenue. We had two huge cakes made. One in the shape of the number seven and the other in the shape of the number five. Placing 37 candles on one cake and 38 on the other and lighting them was scary. We had about 30 invited guests from the church and some of daddy's retired friends. He was excited to see his old police buddies and thrilled that they had survived Katrina. Still one year later, many of the people who came were still scattered across the country and were only in town for daddy's party. I invited a co-worker who was my dad's age from Operation HOPE. His wife had made some Pralines. We all had a great time.

One year and one month had gone by and most parts of the City of New Orleans still looked as if Katrina just happened. Baton Rouge was super crowded. Baton Rouge is the capitol of Louisiana. It is approximately 90 miles west of New Orleans.

So there I was at our very first meeting…the Small Rental Property Repair Program. Anxious to get started and anxious to help all of those who were affected, not just in my hometown New Orleans, but in the entire State of Louisiana. There were about 13 of us at the round table. There were about 12 Caucasian males and females. I was the *only* African-American. As ideas were discussed on how to implement the program, and where to have the people from New Orleans go to apply for assistance with the Road Home Program, someone had a bright idea. *"Let's have the main office near the Stennis Space Center." "Yeah!"* Someone else said. *"Those people are going to come with guns." "What people?"* I interjected. *"Do you know that's an hour and twenty minutes away?! The most damage was done in New Orleans. You haven't answered my question sir, what people are you referring to?"*

Virginia's comment to me when she first met me was beginning to make a lot of sense now. Whoever coined the phrase "Hindsight is 20/20" knew exactly what they were talking about. *"Who are you?,"* someone asked. *"I'm Zelia. Who are you?"* Another associate at the table stepped in and said, *"Why don't we all go 'round robin' and introduce ourselves. Let's all tell us your names, where you're from, and what's your favorite food to eat."* I figured it was the second question that was the important factor here. I'm sure they could give a damn as to what I liked to eat. People can be so transparent at times. As everyone said where they were from, I noticed someone taking notes…just jotting down the places we were from. Some groups are skilled at trying to create diversions too. Trying to linger on the foods that people said they liked to eat, when it was my turn to go, it was crystal clear that I was the only one from New Orleans. *"I thought you were from Houston?"* someone said. The meeting made me start to doubt that there would be an office in New Orleans. It was already decided that we would have an office in Metairie or Kenner and one in Slidell. Metairie and Kenner didn't have nearly as much damage as New Orleans did and we're sitting there talking about not having an office in the main ravaged section of town. *"I was told that there would be an office in New Orleans. Are you saying that this isn't the case?"* *"Everything hasn't been ironed out yet. We may have to put some people in Kenner and some in Slidell."*

"First of all, the <u>main</u> office should be in New Orleans. Most of the people who were affected won't have transportation to go to an office near the Stennis Space Center or anywhere in Mississippi. Not only have their homes been affected, but so have their cars. You make <u>these people</u>, as you call them, have to travel to another state just to get assistance with everything that they've been through I wouldn't blame them for bringing a gun! Logistically speaking, no one here today bothered to conduct any research before coming to this meeting. I'd like to know why a discussion took place to have the main office in another state when the greatest population affected resides in New Orleans?"

As we were developing the program, Virginia began to purposely leave me off of important compliance emails. Virginia was right. I didn't look like any of them or think like them either. I began to think back about that Fortune Teller. Could this too have been in the cards? Can things get any worse?

Throughout the entire meeting, there was one mind of reason. There was a gentleman who sided with me and said, *"She's right! What are they going to do, catch a taxi?"* I'm sure it took a lot of courage for him to speak the truth and against his counterparts. I felt like an outcast and that the people sitting at the table with me thought less of the people who were from

New Orleans. Now, I've been to meetings where people got yelled at and cussed at. But at the end of the day, we would take away something that was capable of being executed. Our first meeting, on day one, was a sign of what was to come regarding the execution of the Road Home program...total chaos.

The next couple of days another employee named Karen was hired. She had never worked in a grants management program before and had no housing background. Frankly speaking, she was just happy to be there.

Later on, I got word later that the main office would be in New Orleans. It shouldn't have taken a rocket scientist to figure out that this would be for the best considering the massive devastation that took place there.

As more people were hired, we began sharing our offices with one another. I also got word that I would be gone by the end of the year. The guy who had my back in the first meeting asked me if we could share offices together. Hesitant at first, I told him, *"Sure."* Frank's background was in banking. He was married, and like myself, had two children—a daughter that was married and a son about to go to high school. Frank didn't have the arrogant and pompous attitudes like so many of the other associates. He talked about his children a lot and all the family gatherings that took place with him and his wife. He and I would share information to benefit the company and the thousands who were affected. He knew that I liked Pralines and one day brought some in that his wife had made for me. I jokingly asked Frank if he was married to a "sista" because those pralines tasted like Loretta's from "Loretta's Authentic Pralines" on North Rampart in New Orleans. Frank and I became good friends.

In a couple of weeks, someone from New Orleans was hired to be the Environmentalist—the second African-American. Like me, she had worked for the City of New Orleans. She lived in the Gentilly area; down the street from the Lakefront. We both stayed at the same hotel in Baton Rouge right off College Drive. Elaine started catching a ride with me to work every day. She and I became close friends. She shared an office with Bill, Virginia's friend. Bill missed a lot of days at work and would take vacations to Costa Rica.

After working downtown and everyone being cramped up in each other's offices, we were all told to report to our new offices located on Goodwood. We would be stationed there until the offices in Slidell, Kenner, and New Orleans were ready.

As more employees came aboard, the 'round robin exercise became all too familiar and an inside joke. When it was Karen's turn, she proudly said, *"I'm extremely glad to be here and I just want everyone here to know that I don't mind kissing up to any supervisor's ass."* With no hesitation in her voice, Karen had divulged that she would do anything to gain upward mobility in the Road Home program. There's one in every workplace. With Karen's straight forwardness, we didn't have to figure out who held the title of ass-kisser. Umph! I'll never understand that type of mind.

Karen's eagerness to move up, by any means necessary, was unbelievable. When we moved over to our new offices on Goodwood, she became my office mate along with another new hire. Once again, we were beginning to get overcrowded. When she wasn't working, which was most of the time, she was snacking…all day long. Karen had shared with me, Elaine and the other office member that she met an "older" man online. They emailed each other throughout the day…about as much as she snacked. You would have thought she was working for a 1-900 number or something. Though, in spite of her insatiable ability to kiss ass, Karen was hilarious! Working that close with one another in one office, we all soon became to know the lives of each other. She told us that her sister met her husband online and that she was destined to meet hers that way too. After knowing the older man for about one month, Karen decided to allow him to come and visit her at the hotel where we all lived whose tab was being paid for by the State. Elaine and I tried to talk some sense into Karen to let her know how dangerous that could be. It looked like common logic was definitely a hard commodity to come by inside the walls of ICF and the Road Home Program.

Karen was insistent on letting this man she had never met or even seen before come and live with her. She said that he lived in Florida and was driving or catching a bus down to Baton Rouge. It sounded to me like he needed a place to stay. Karen was a little over 300 pounds and that was on her first day on the job. With all the snacking and double lunches she took; well, let's just say that she didn't want to email the "older" gentleman a picture of herself. While she may not have looked like a box of chocolates, Karen did have a pleasant personality. She told us that their many conversations made them both realize that they were meant for each other. Elaine and I wanted to know when he was coming in town so that we could check him out from afar or even call the Po-Po's just in case he was a crazed man. He must have been crazy to deal with Karen. *We* already knew she wasn't playing with a full deck. It was completely normal for Karen to tell the manager at the hotel to leave the key for a stranger to get in her apartment until she got off from work. Was this something that only white people did? 'Cause black folks don't give their house keys to their own relatives.

I think Elaine and I were more anxious for the arrival of Karen's newfound beau than Karen was. It was a little after lunch time. Karen's boyfriend had arrived to Baton Rouge and was waiting for her to come home to greet him.

The next day, Elaine and I ate breakfast in the lobby and drove to work. Normally, we'd see Karen in the lobby too. Perhaps she was sleeping in late, we thought. We were hoping everything was okay. An hour had gone by and Karen wasn't at work yet. Elaine was the one who had Karen's cell phone number. Elaine said she called and left a couple of messages on Karen's voicemail. I told Elaine that if Karen didn't come in by noon, we should call the police. This girl had never seen this man in person or online. She only had his cell phone number and had only talked to him on the cell phone a couple of times. Ohh, uhh-uhh! I pray I never become that desperate for a man.

Karen finally graced us with her presence. We told her that in one more hour an all points bulletin would have been put out on her ass. She put down her purse, then her lunch, then snacks, and her second lunch on her desk. She began to give us the 411 on what happened yesterday when she went home. Karen said that as she walked closer to her apartment, she smelled something good coming from the inside. Her friend had made her a nice home cooked meal. She said that they sat around and exchanged information and the time just went by really quickly. That was awfully nice of him. She said they simply decided to sleep in.

We all wanted so badly to see how this guy looked; we couldn't wait to see him. We asked Karen when were they going out again. This was so we could see them coming out of her apartment together. Karen told us they were going to church that Sunday. They were going to church and this guy wanted to meet her Pastor. Karen barely knew the preacher herself. She wasn't from Baton Rouge. This guy was surely working fast.

While curiosity got the best of me, as Sunday came, I made an exit to my car, which was also parked next to Karen's. Much to my surprise, there were other employees in the parking lot too, as I wasn't the only curious one. Elaine was in her car too. An elderly man or Karen's dad was getting out of her car. She didn't tell us her dad was in town too! Then we saw Karen walking towards the car. She spoke to us and introduced her… her…her new friend!!! Karen's friend was older than my dad and could barely walk. He had some medical contraption connected to his body. What the hell?! Was he for real?! Was she for real?! By now, I was having another Scooby Doo moment. I had seen it all. See, this is why you don't date online. She didn't want to email her picture to him and obviously he didn't want to email his picture to her. I'm surprised that he knew how to use a computer. I'm sure several forms of technology were invented since he was born. Ohh, uhh-uhh!

When we got to work the next day, Karen said that she was having second thoughts about this guy. She said that he had brought all of his belongings with him. He wanted her to marry him. Well, she wanted to be like her sister and marry someone from the internet didn't she? Now was her chance. At least now we knew we didn't have to worry about Karen's safety. This guy couldn't hurt a fly.

As the holidays quickly approached, I received numerous policy guideline manuals that would change on a weekly basis— sometimes daily. As soon as I would get through reading and highlighting some procedural concerns, I would receive a new manual and have to start all over again. Policy would change so rapidly that it became known in the workplace as the "five-minute rule," meaning; every five minutes the rules of the program would change. I swear it was reading all of those manuals that messed up my eyes and now I need glasses.

Karen finally decided to put her friend out and told him he would have to go find somewhere else to stay.

While we were in our office one day, Karen told me to slowly turn around to see if I knew the person standing in the window looking at me. Elaine and Karen both stared at this strange man while I continued to type on my computer. *"Hurry, turn around and look! He's just starring at you!"* I turned around and there he was. I had no idea who this person was or why he was staring at me like he hadn't seen a woman before. You would have thought that he just got out of prison. *"Okay, it's going on two minutes and he's still starring. Anyone know who this guy is?"* Elaine said. Elaine was the eldest of us all. She went out and asked this man to identify himself. He introduced himself as Waldo, and said it was his first day on the job. Much to our surprise, we would later find out at the silly 'round robin that Waldo was friends with Bill and Virginia, and was hired to work alongside Elaine. Lucky Elaine!

The very next day, Waldo asked me out to lunch. I told him that I didn't take lunches. *"So what about dinner?"* he asked. *"I'm not interested in going to dinner with you or anywhere else. Aren't you married?"* I asked, as I noticed a ring on his left hand. Waldo walked away and went towards his office. That afternoon, Waldo came back as I was walking and said, *"I'd like to take you to Baskin Robbins for some ice cream and lick you all over."* Waldo was 62 years old and clearly a lunatic. Trying not to go 9th Ward on him, I did anyway and told Waldo that he was old enough to be my great, great, great grandfather!! Where did these people come from? They were like office rejects. And they all worked for the Road Home Program?! OHH, UHH-UHH!

Momma and daddy bought another home on the Westbank. Our family home was completely in ruins. The neighborhood in the 9th Ward remained deserted. I still don't know where everyone went. The neighbors that we grew up with next door moved to Detroit. Mrs. Moore's husband had already passed years ago. She went to live with her oldest daughter, Belle.

Momma and daddy had to replace every piece of furniture. This Christmas would be the first time since Katrina that we all would be spending it together back home with our family. There were still no department stores open, one year later, in New Orleans. I would buy momma Christmas decorations from Baton Rouge on my days off.

It was my favorite time of the year. Alex and Torey drove up to Baton Rouge to stay with me every other weekend. They liked to make waffles on Saturday mornings at the hotel. This visit though, they were especially excited because they knew that I would be coming home to them for the holidays. After packing all my belongings, I checked out of the hotel, and we all headed to New Orleans.

QUATRE
THE WARNING

AFTER BRINGING IN THE NEW YEAR, I WAS BEGINNING to get settled in at my new office in New Orleans on Poydras Street. It was rumored that Waldo would be stationed at the Kenner office.

Each week new staff members were being added to the program and particularly at the New Orleans office. After hearing that I was on staff as the Compliance agent and monitor for the program, a few old school buddies that had also been hired with the Road Home that I hadn't seen in years came by my office to say hello and catch up on what each other had been doing since we graduated. A few weeks later, one of my old school mates pulled me to the side to divulge that Bill was having private meetings with them making disparaging and negative remarks about me. That same week, another new hire that I didn't know also asked to speak with me and shared the exact same remarks about Bill that my old school buddy had shared previously. When I asked the unknown new hire why he felt Bill was doing this, he said that it made him feel as if Bill was trying to get the employees to dislike me before they had an opportunity to get to know me. I asked the new hire who else was in the meeting. He said there were three other new hires. I then thanked him for sharing the information.

I spoke with Elaine about this and she suggested I call Bill out on this. Bill was no longer our Director. His position had been down-graded and his good buddy Virginia was now the Director—all within a matter of a couple of months. No one really knew what Bill's new title was anymore, as he originally started off with one of the highest paid salaries in the Road Home program.

I told the Small Rental Property Program's Operations Manager that I wanted to call a meeting with him and Bill. At the meeting, Bill didn't deny that he was defaming my character and talking to the new hires negatively about me. Ain't that some stuff! He would eventually apologize in the meeting and try to cover up his remarks creating another diversion by telling me that he wanted to be just like me driving a Benz and that he thought I was a very professional person. What was he talking about? The only person who had seen the car I drove was Virginia. He even commented on me wearing pearl necklaces and dressing in suits. Bill said that he felt that I was a professional and did my job properly but that there were some people in Baton Rouge that wanted to get rid of me. The new Operations Manager asked me to stay behind when Bill left the meeting. The Manager then thanked me for calling the meeting and sharing the information. Bill was purposely going around having meetings with new employees making slanderous remarks about me. His negative actions would have made it extremely difficult for me to perform my job duties as the Compliance Specialist and obtain necessary information from new hires as it related to the effectiveness of the program. He went on to say that things would have been very different for me the following week had I not requested the meeting with him in on it, as managers in the Baton Rouge office were planning for my exit from the program. He said that it was all making more sense to him. He said from what he had witnessed, I was an extremely professional person and that the remarks that Bill was making would have made employees distrust me. He was absolutely right! New hires would have been apprehensive to discuss their office application procedures with me in order for me to compare policy with what was physically being put into practice in accordance with HUD's regulations and guidelines.

While the majority of the top personnel had high paying jobs, they started interviewing nonexempt employees to retrieve documents and collect applications. Many of the top personnel lacked intellectual capacity and critical management skills. Nonexempt employees are the ones who can get overtime pay whenever they work more than a 40 hour work week. These employees would be the face of New Orleans and their salaries would be tremendously less than that of the top echelon in Baton Rouge. Instead of calling them Customer Service Representatives, their titles would be Housing Advisors and Housing Counselors. It was a clever marketing strategy to place African-Americans as the greeter at the door to be the "face" and the "spokesperson" for the program. BP did the same thing with the oil spill on the Gulf Coast, while behind the scenes directors received multiple unimaginable salaries, we ignored the fact that a greater devastation was occurring right before our own eyes; the beginning of gentrification.

They wanted the citizens who needed assistance to be able to relate with the workers on the 7th floor (Small Rental Property Program) and 9th floor (Homeowner Assistance Program). Unfortunately, these Advisors and Counselors however, were not the decision makers. Though some of the sweetest people you ever want to meet, many of them had never been involved with any federally funded grants management program. Their titles were well crafted by senior management to "sound" as if they were making decisions concerning the citizens' applications and the overall application process. For example, a "Counselor" is usually someone who provides direction or advice regarding a decision or course of action. This person is oftentimes professionally trained or licensed and may have supervisory duties. A "Counselor" can also be someone who pleads cases in courts such as an attorney. However at each citywide workshop, these counselors were given direction to specifically say that they "could not give advice or provide direction" to the citizens seeking assistance with their application process. An "Advisor" has a greater authority than that of a counselor in that it is someone who is not just a licensed or trained professional, but is considered an expert at their craft and has a discernment of insight that others may lack. An "Advisor" is definitely the "go to" person to get advice and guidance. These Advisors and Counselors simply *collected* the applications and supporting documents and *mailed* them to a post office box where it would then be retrieved and brought to the office on Goodwood in Baton Rouge. Advisors and Counselors were completely unaware that they were being used as the middle man. These proud men and women were there to work with the program to honestly assist in helping the tens of thousands of individuals who needed Road Home assistance. Placing these titles upon the employees was a clever way to avert the blame off senior management in Baton Rouge. This charade to deflect blame, however, wouldn't last long.

Not surprisingly, some older male managers were taking advantage of young, female staff members. They would take them out for drinks and make promises regarding upward mobility within the company. Waldo who had been married multiple times and was currently married at the time was one of those managers. In less than two months, his title quickly rose from being under Elaine who was the expert in Historical Preservation/Environmental to being over Elaine. He was now Deputy Operations Manager of the Small Rental Property Program. I had often wondered who did he blow to get that spot. I doubt if he knew how to even *spell* the word preservation. He certainly wasn't preserving himself for his wife back home in Florida. Unfortunately, some of these young girls were given more unwarranted attention by grumpy old men in the workplace than they were probably given at home by their baby daddy's.

The two men that led the office on the 7th floor at the Poydras site were the proud managers of the rental program. They were just as surprised to hold those titles as most of us were. The two of them put together couldn't follow directions on how to unfold a lawn chair, yet they were Bat Man and Robin of the Road Home program charged with coming to the aid of thousands of landlords and owners of multi-family dwellings.

The Road Home

BUILDING A SAFER,
STRONGER, SMARTER LOUISIANA

NEWS RELEASE
FOR IMMEDIATE RELEASE

Contact:
Carol Hector-Harris
225-242-1041

Dwight Cunningham
225-242-1035

RENTAL PROPERTY OWNER ENCOURAGED TO APPLY TO
***THE ROAD HOME* SMALL RENTAL PROPERTY PRORAM**

BATON ROUGE, La., January 29, 2007 – Today, *The Road Home* launches its Small Rental Property program, providing incentives to encourage property owners to rebuild much needed affordable residents still displaced by the hurricanes.

Before the storms, many low-and moderate-income working families lived in single-family homes, doubles, and small multi-unit building. For the most part, these were owned and operated by small-scale rental property owners. Through a series of competitive application rounds, *The Road Home* rental program will provide incentives as forgivable loans that are forgiven in stages over time. By providing an incentive for owners to rebuild their rental properties and requiring them to keep rents affordable, the Small Rental Property program is helping bring back reasonably priced rental properties in the most storm damaged areas.

"There is a great need for affordable rental options for our residents. By providing incentives to owners of rental properties, we are rebuilding our neighborhoods and offering housing options that people can actually afford," stated Calvin Parker of the Office of Community Development.

The program will offer awards through a series of competitive application rounds to ensure incentives are available to those owners who need it most. This initial round is targeted towards small-scale owners with up to 20 rental units. Larger property owners will be given an opportunity to apply in later rounds, but the program will continue to prioritize small-scale applicants. The amount of the incentive an owner may receive will depend on the affordability of rents the property owner is will to charge. Owner occupants of three-and four-unit properties are strongly encouraged to apply.

Small Rental Property Program
Page 2

Starting today, applications for small-scale and owner-occupant property owners are available for Round 1 of the program. This first round will remain opened and accepting applications until March 15, 2007.

Some of the funding has been specified for nonprofit organizations offering a longer term affordability and supportive housing. These applications will be available starting February 12 through March 22.

To be eligible, applicants must have owned a one-to four-unit rental property located in one of the 13 parishes hardest hit by the storms: Acadia, Calcasieu, Cameron, Iberia, Jefferson, Orleans, Plaquemines, St. Bernard, St. Tammany, Tangipahoa, Terrebonne, Vermilion and Washington. All eligibility criteria can be found online at *www.road2LA.org/rental* or by call *The Road Home* call center at **1.888.ROAD.2.LA (1.888.762.3252). TTY callers use 711 relay or 1.800.846.5277**.

An application can be requested by calling 1.888.ROAD.2.LA or visiting *www.road2LA.org*. Completed applications should be mailed to P.O. Box 4729, Baton Rouge, LA 70821-1182. If an applicant is unable to complete an application in time for the Round 1 deadline, they are encouraged to apply in a later application round. There will be multiple rounds of funding with Round 2 opening in late April.

Last fall, the State launched a separate program to spur development of mixed-income and low-income housing through tax incentives and grants. The Low Income Housing Tax Credit (LIHTC) program is expected to spur private investment in more than 15,000 rental units, including 5,000 units in a mixed-income setting. This development will add to the construction boom and help address a post-storm shortage of affordable rental properties.

The Road Home program is designed to help Louisiana residents affected by Hurricane Katrina or Rita get back into their homes as quickly and fairly as possible. Working together, Governor Kathleen Babineaux Blanco, the Louisiana Recovery Authority, the Office of Community Development and the Louisiana Legislature created The Small Rental Property program. The program, designed for one-to four-unit rental properties, provides incentives to owners offering affordable work force rental housing for returning residents.

For more information on The Small Rental Property program or to request an application, visit *www.road2LA.org/rental* or call 1.888.ROAD.2.LA (1.888.762.3252). TTY callers use 711 relay or 1.800.846.5277.

As much training that went on under the pretense of implementing the program, one would have thought that the program would have been executed more efficiently. Training took place every week with Advisors, Counselors, and Rehab Specialists. Sometimes trainings took place more frequently. Just when everyone knew their roles, policy regarding the program would change basically every five minutes. The inside joke of the *"five minute rule"* all of a sudden was not funny anymore.

While the Press Release and the news media outlets stated that the Small Rental Property Program was opening on January 29, 2007, it was pure rhetoric and an out-right lie, as the doors to the 7th floor stayed closed and the Operations Manager walked from office to office telling Advisors and Counselors to keep their doors to their offices closed and not to speak with any applicant if one comes in. *"What the hell are you doing?"* I asked the Operations Manager. *"Why are these doors locked?"* *"Management in Baton Rouge wants us to simply take the applications from the applicants until further notice,"* he said. *"And did you ask them why? They just did a Press Release that the program is open for business."* His response was an emphatic, *"No."* *"Well, if you're supposed to be the Operations Manager, you need to do just that…run this operation, there are people out there counting on this program for them to survive."* As Martin Luther King said in 1963, *"Nothing in all the world is more dangerous than sincere ignorance and conscientious stupidity."* I am so glad that I have intellect and confidence to never be a mere token for any company, I thought to myself. I'll never understand that type of mind. I'm too smart to be a token or what I call a "cover-up" and too skilled to use my talent for wrongdoing. I've come to learn that some African-Americans feel threatened to simply speak the truth in the workplace. If telling the truth means that I have to be on welfare for the rest of my life because someone's going to fire me; then I will be on welfare for the rest of my life. *"Knowing who you are is the foundation of everything great."* Jay-Z

The Road Home was beginning to be the *Road To Nowhere.* OPEN in words only, no one knew the charades that were being enacted within the second program. Thousands of people's lives and livelihood were at stake. Why was management deliberately having multiple unnecessary trainings? Train them on what…how to keep their doors shut? Why were they stalling with issuing out the grant awards to the citizens who were counting on them the most? Shouldn't the trainings have helped the program and not hinder its progress? My philosophy is that you can train anyone. Were these trainings and stall tactics a disguise or another diversion to justify the request for more funding to run the program that really hadn't begun? What was the purpose of keeping the doors closed for one week and why wasn't Virginia returning calls to answer that question? With all the terminology and buzz words floating around such as *"Round*

1 and Round 2," who knew that the applicants would feel as if they were in the "boxing ring" as they had to constantly fight with the continuous changing of policy and procedures surrounding the program while simultaneously maintaining their stamina to fight for their own emotional survival, as it was going on two years since Katrina hit.

In the meantime, with all the promises made by the two male managers of the Small Rental Property Repair Program to the younger female employees regarding higher positions, morale in the workplace hit an all time low…and we hadn't even opened our doors to the public yet. The young female employees started jocking each other for better offices and demands to be "team leaders" from Waldo and the Operations Manager who were promising them everything. The younger female employees were quickly evolving into the characters like the "Lord of the Flies."

Then on February 19, 2007, Waldo purposely left me out of a strategic meeting regarding ongoing changes in the policies and procedures of the Small Rental Property Repair Program. I forwarded my concern to the Operations Manager and cc'd Virginia in Baton Rouge. I was told by Waldo that I would not be needed to work in my role as QA/QC and that a younger female employee with no degree would be taking my place as lead. The email I forwarded was entitled, "Compliance Process & Forced Lack of Inclusion." It would be one of many more emails to come that I would send to them concerning management's deliberate scheme to prevent me from discovering the secret that lurked in the offices of the infamous Road Home program.

In less than a month, the Operations Manager who said things were beginning to make sense to him regarding management's attempt to get rid of me began assisting management with obstructing me from performing my job duties.

It was March 13, 2007, and whenever I would enter the offices of an Advisor or Counselor to check on the performance of the program, I was given silent treatment and then told by one senior Advisor that the Operations Manager told him not to talk to me or answer any questions. I confronted the Operations Manager about this and he apologized later on that evening saying that he was under a lot of pressure and alluded to the fact that Virginia was the one behind it all. He begged me not to write any correspondences to senior management and assured me that it wouldn't happen again. Was Virginia's statement to me when she first met me filled with racial overtones? Is that what this is about? She hired the wrong *colored* person to be the compliance agent for the New Orleans territory? Was she that disappointed that I didn't look the way she thought I ought to? I know I've been told numerous times throughout my life that I sound White over the phone, but give me a break!! Most importantly, were these people who were aiding whoever was behind this charade to get rid of me getting paid to do this? In one month it will be 2011, and some groups in America are still preoccupied as to whether you're Black or White. The Operations Manager also went and apologized to the elder Advisor. That Advisor would later become someone who shared information with me regarding the program's demise.

One and a half years later, that same elder Advisor would forward this statement to my attorney regarding federal violations against ICF and the Road Home program.

Date: Tue, 7 Oct 2008 13:57:42 -0700
From: Elder Advisor
To: Attorney for Federal Court
Subject: Elder Advisor's statement

My name is XXXXX XXXXXXX and I was employed by ICF
as a Housing Advisor with the Road Home Program. This is
statement of an incident that occurred involving myself, Lisa
Brown and my manager at the time, XXXXXX XXXXXXX. It
was my understanding that Mrs Lisa Brown was responsible for
'Quality Control and Assurance' of the program and that it was
her duty to make sure that the staff complied with the policies
and procedures of the Road Home Program. A staff meeting
was conducted by Mr. XXXXXXX that was not attended by
Mrs. Brown. During that particular staff meeting, Mr. XXXXXXX
spoke about some policy matters. After the meeting I spoke
with Mrs. Brown about a particular policy that Mr. XXXXXXX
had discussed. I do not recall the specific policy matter that had
concerned me. I thought that she could provide some clarity
on that particular policy, since she was responsible for quality
control would probably have been aware of the policy. She
stated that she would get confirmation of the policy and get back
with me. Mr. XXXXXXX came in to my office later that day and
instructed me 'not to go Mrs. Brown anymore with questions
about policy and procedure'. I explained to him that I spoke to

Mrs. Brown in her capacity as the 'Quality Control' person for clarification of the policy that he discussed in the staff meeting. He reiterated to me, 'not to go to her about policy matters'. I told him that I would comply with his instruction. Mr. XXXXXXX came back in to my office later that day and apologized for his prior visit and retracted his previous instruction not to discuss policy matters with Mrs. Brown. He did not give any reason or explanation for his behavior and I did not ask for one. I do not know how Mr. XXXXXXX became aware of my discussion with Mrs. Brown as I did not inform him of that discussion.

After about a month of being opened to the public, I received over 100 emails from discouraged Advisors, Counselors, and Rehab Specialists making suggestions on how to improve the program in their quest to get attention from Virginia and others in Baton Rouge.

Every chance that Waldo could get, if he wasn't walking behind me singing, *"I'm not Lisa..."* he was blatantly holding meetings with other personnel leaving me off of emails concerning meetings and trainings. After a few times of this, Elaine began to either forward me the emails that had my name left off or call me from her cell phone to let me know where the meetings were taking place. Eventually, more employees were noticing the deliberate acts by management to purposely leave me out and began to share pertinent office information.

On March 23, 2007, I forwarded my weekly report to Virginia and the Operations Manager outlining constraints in my department regarding not being included in on meetings, emails, and conference calls. Virginia remained very quiet through it all.

If that wasn't enough, Rehab Specialists received unnecessary trainings daily and were never given the opportunity to perform their job duties and inspect a home. Some of the specialists became livid and felt used. They began to leave or quit the program to go back to their hometown. They felt that the program was a joke and was upset that they had wasted their time and money to move to the city to help out; only to find out that they were there under false pretense. We all would later discover that a contract had already been given to HGI to conduct inspections on the properties. Why would there be a need to have titled inspectors in-house and contracted titled inspectors on the outside? The more I found out, the more complicated the secret became to crack. Would I ever discover the truth behind the disaster within a disaster?

Well, stupid is as stupid does, and with Waldo on the prowl it would only be a matter of time before he would mess up and be viewed as a public nuisance. He did exactly that on March 27, 2007 at a meeting he called where he made disparaging comments regarding the residents of New Orleans in front of over 63 employees saying that everyone from New Orleans was *"dumb and stupid."* He stated that the City of New Orleans was crafted by dumb and stupid people. An older Caucasian female employee began to get emotional at the meeting and cried. You see, many of the Advisors and Counselors were victims themselves and also needed assistance. They came to work in hostile conditions at the Road Home only to return to their temporary homes, FEMA trailers, which presented a more unfavorable condition with leaking ceilings and alleged formaldehyde. Waldo was totally unbecoming of a professional. When he wasn't trying to get some ass, he was condescending to the staff members, and generated inappropriate conflict amongst employees. First, it was the Outreach staff member from the

Baton Rouge office who made negative remarks saying, *"It's the culture for those people in New Orleans to turn things in late"* to the repugnant comments made by Waldo the following week that everyone in New Orleans was *"dumb and stupid."* That Tuesday, Waldo showed the entire staff that he was definitely, as my dad would say, not an "in-betweener." He would go down in history as being one of the most memorable individuals one would encounter...and not for his academic acumen. I then recommended Sensitivity Training take place with all superiors.

Two days later, Waldo was no longer with the company. When asked what happened to him, management in Baton Rouge would say they couldn't give out information regarding one's personnel records. ICF had finally decided to conduct an investigation after a string of damage had already been done. Prior to that, not only was Waldo allowed to work in the same department as his son, he was also allowed to supervise him. Waldo didn't know how to use a computer or fax and would get other women to write or type correspondences for him. Waldo must have been good at something; but what that was remained a mystery. It would be months later that I would discover the secret about Waldo.

March 30, 2007, I received a Meeting Agenda without it acknowledging my name and position with the company and no assignments given to me to perform. All of my assignments were given to outside Compliance agents. It was as if I was no longer employed with the program on paper and there was no other compliance expert located at the New Orleans office.

People were being flown in from all over the U.S. to work with the Road Home program and given senior management titles with unprecedented salaries. However, some of them had prejudiced overtones and attitudes towards the citizens of New Orleans which made for very little comfort for a productive work environment.

With their biggest flunky and not so good deed doer gone, management in Baton Rouge began to step it up with getting rid of me. I discovered that Virginia was the mastermind behind this entire ordeal. While I took off on Good Friday, Virginia sent an email to Human Resources directing them to take *"action"* and get rid of me. Like the rest of them because she was not savvy at using the computer, she inadvertently copied me along with the others involved in on the scheme. Thanks to her misfortune in computer 101, I now knew who all the key players were, and she was definitely the head honcho orchestrating it all.

Exactly two days after I reported Waldo and one day after he resigned, Virginia, the Program Director and good friend of Waldo, emailed me a *"final written warning."* Now to an intellectual, the word "final" means last, end, the last of a series of warnings. Receiving this was very surprising in that I had not received any verbal or written warnings before this one. Throughout it all, I had to keep reminding myself that I was not dealing with any scholarly people there though. The warning stated that I had missed training. Were these the trainings that they were purposely leaving me out of? Was that their orchestrated scheme? Were they deliberately leaving me out of meetings and trainings so that I could be written up and they build a paper trail on a lie? This was one of the oldest schemes in the books of discrimination and retaliation. I guess they felt I'd either get tired of the road blocks and shenanigans and just throw in the towel and quit. They felt that because I didn't go along with the damaged product that they were offering to the public, being on the inside would pose a threat to what they really came to do.

It was beginning to make sense to me now when Virginia met me and said that she didn't expect me to look the way I looked. Because my cell phone number was still a Houston area code, she probably also thought I was from Houston and not from New Orleans. They were definitely up to something from the beginning, and I would be the one to find out.

Going back on his word, the next day the Operations Manager told the staff not to forward weekly reports to me anymore. Unbeknownst to management, the Housing Advisors and Housing Counselors were losing confidence in them and had already begun to confide in me. They too wanted to assist more with helping the citizens and landlords with receiving their appropriate grant awards and felt that they were being refrained from doing that. I then filed a grievance internally and also with EEOC.

Who knew that almost a year after dealing with the destruction of my home on the Lakefront that I would embark upon a sea of corruption within ICF and the Road Home program as Compliance Specialist.

Having experienced the deficiencies, ineptness, and the debacle with monitoring the administering of funds within the program, it would only be a matter of time before the contracted company imploded. In time and in greed, they always do. Because of the toxic political corruption, and *business as usual* attitudes that permeated Louisiana and the City of New Orleans pre-Katrina, cronyism, gross mismanagement, and discrimination on all levels continued to take place while a major American city drowned. More than 250,000 people were forced out of their homes and a little over 80% of the city was attempting to recover from being under water. All recovery efforts thereafter were identical to watching people "build an airplane while in flight."

CINQ
BEAUCOUP (BO-KOO) MISMANAGEMENT
(Defined as "an abundance of mismanagement") French word

IT WAS EVIDENT THAT I WAS DEALING WITH SOME members on the management team that was ethically bankrupt. As the dedicated Advisors and Counselors got deeper into receiving applications concerning the rental program, massive reports of mismanagement hit the airwaves.

In an attempt to do damage control, directors from the Baton Rouge office came to visit the New Orleans office. Only management had seen the people from Baton Rouge, as we were hired shortly after ICF had been awarded the contract to run the Road Home program and we lived in the Baton Rouge area before our offices were ready in New Orleans.

The elder Advisor was very knowledgeable when it came to political interest groups in America and was well versed surrounding major events that took place within American history.

Engaging in conversations like that appealed to the nerdy side of me. He, Elaine, and I would talk about all sorts of things; particularly during lunch time. I never went out for lunch so I would get Elaine's lunch for her from the 1st floor and we would all sit in her office to chat.

In addition to Elaine, now with the advisors and counselors alerting me to the meetings that I was not invited to, as I entered one meeting, there was a flip chart on an easel with a heading that said, *"Awsome Job!"* As the entire staff of Housing Counselors and Housing Advisors in the room yelled out, *"the e, the e,"* alerting the Operations Manager that the word was missing an "e;" he then scratched out the "e" at the end of the word I guess thinking that because it was silent it didn't belong there. It now read, "Awsom Job!" Go figure. I was surrounded by an "awsom" group of managers who were supervising the largest paid contract in America's history. Yet they were the ones that said the people from New Orleans were *dumb and stupid*.

Meanwhile, I was in the process of dealing with my own home on the Lakefront. I had given Countrywide a check in the amount of $50,000 to put towards my mortgage loan balance. I had owned the home for almost 15 years. While applicants had their battles with the Road Home program, I had my own mêlées (from the French mêlée) with Countrywide Home Mortgage.

After documenting conversations and forwarding certified letters to over 100 Customer Service Reps at the company, including the CEO, I began contacting Attorney Generals in California and Louisiana, the Federal Trade Commission, Securities Exchange Commission, Better Business Bureau of Tri-Counties, and other agencies that monitor mortgage companies. As a housing consultant, I also keep up with housing market trends.

On July 7, 2007, I forwarded a certified correspondence to Angelo Mozillo, then President/CEO of Countrywide, and cc'd Edmund Brown, Attorney General of California, Charles Foti, Attorney General for Louisiana, Louisiana Office of Financial Institutions, and Daniel Whitehead, BBB of the Tri-Counties, alerting them of Countrywide's unorthodox practice of keeping customer's checks and not applying it to loan mortgage balances and also my forecast of approximately "1.1 million flood of foreclosures" about to take place in America, as studies were showing that each 1% rise or drop in housing prices would translate into an increase or decrease of roughly 70,000 in foreclosures. In addition to Countrywide holding on to my check, they would consistently offer me *home equity loans* in an effort to increase my balance. Their goal was not to allow victims of the storm to pay off or pay down their mortgages.

Countrywide was purposely holding checks that I forwarded to their office to go towards my mortgage payments and recklessly allowing interest and penalties to build up for two consecutive years. Countrywide's mission *"to help people achieve and preserve homeownership"* was as questionable as the platinum blonde hair on its CEO's head.

Meanwhile at the office, when Virginia and the others arrived to our offices on Poydras, it was the elder Advisor who saw them first. He called me on the phone from his office down the hallway saying, *"Liiii-sa! Have you seen them yet?"* The elder Advisor had a distinguished voice. He spoke slowly and deliberately. He had a distinctive voice that sounded like Vincent Price. He was extremely articulate and well versed. *"Liiii-sa! Liiii-sa! You're kidding me right? You've got to be kidding me, right!!,* he said. *"Somebody's wearing flip flops! Liiii-sa! Are these the people calling the shots and running this program? Liiii-sa! Which one is Virginia?"* he asked curiously. *"She's the one wearing the flip flops,"* I replied. The elder Advisor dropped the phone. I was laughing so hard at the comments he made that I didn't realize he had hung up the phone and was standing in my office doorway closing the door behind him. Looking at me with great concern, the elder Advisor said, *"These people look like they were pulled off the streets...no Liiii-sa ? Is it just me?"* he said as he tried to whisper though still sounding like Vincent Price. *"No it isn't just you. We're making negative headlines in the news and the workers are beginning to have several questions about how the program is being run. And because I'm not standing behind what they're doing, I'm being singled out."* Virginia and the others walked around and toured the offices as if they were on a field trip. As the advisors and counselors met the top guns, there was much interaction in each of their offices as they were scampering around too trying to figure out how these individuals could possibly be in charge to run such an important program.

Meetings were then held informing everyone to not wear their badges in public when they were off duty, as the program continued to receive negative headlines in the newspapers and on the local news channels.

After realizing her email mistake, Virginia added a new manager to assist in going after me and harassing me. At first this manager sent emails to her and others telling them how *"disorganized and unproductive"* the trainings were. He would get into heated arguments with them on the program's demise, and cc'd me on those emails. He would later be summoned to report to the Baton Rouge office for a meeting with senior management. He went in as a manager concerned about the mismanagement of the program, and returned to New Orleans reprogrammed as a Stepford Wife with a promotion. I'd like to know where that phone booth is in Baton Rouge so that I can go in with one title and come back out with a higher one and a raise. His energy to speak out on the lackluster of the program ceased. He was now directing anger and harassing tones towards me as he had been promoted when he went to Baton Rouge and was now over me. He directed me to perform duties equivalent to that of a secretary and to cease with conducting quality control on the program. The New Orleans office already had two Administrative Assistants to perform clerical duties.

Elaine started calling me in the mornings as soon as she would arrive to work to check on me to make sure that I was okay. One time, I had my cycle to last for 30 days, and my hair started falling out at the top of my head. I was beginning to get so stressed out from all of the tormenting and harassment that Virginia and her flunkies were dishing out. If I tried to talk to Virginia or the others about Title 24 of the Code of Federal Regulations (CFR), Title VIII and the Fair Housing Act, or any other housing regulations, I was quickly diverted. It was clear that they did not want to engage in any conversation with me concerning the Road Home program. How was I to do any type of quality control being left out of program procedures regarding the Road Home program?

Like the Advisors and Counselors, I began to lose confidence in my superiors and had no other choice but to forward an email to political officials, after other emails were ignored; particularly the one forwarded to Virginia where there were over 100 suggestions received from the people on the floor who actually did the work.

Housing and Urban Development (HUD) residential rehabilitation programs have been around since 1975. So delivering this type of program should have been an easy task. There should have been experienced grants management employees, realtors, settlement title attorneys, real housing appraisers, the City's housing department and other related professionals. Mississippi and Alabama didn't have this type of problem with issuing funds to its citizens.

Leaders Protest Slow New Orleans Recovery
March planned for late April

Leaders Protest Slow New Orleans Recovery

Source: United Press International
Publication date: 2007-04-04

The Rev. Jesse Jackson said he and other black leaders are planning to march in New Orleans to protest the slow pace of rebuilding in the city.

Jackson said the march, planned for April 28 in the 9th Ward, is aimed at protesting the city's pace of recovery that is keeping about 250,000 residents in exile two years after Hurricane Katrina hit the region, The New Orleans Times Picayune reported Wednesday.

The focus has been on the return of the ball club but not the people. Two years later, 250,000 are still in exile. They are not refugees. They are citizens, said Jackson. The 9th Ward remains barren.

Jackson announced the march at a news conference with New Orleans Mayor Ray Nagin, U.S. Rep. Sheila Jackson-Lee, D-Texas, and others leaders.

He said the 9th Ward is a metaphor for neglected urban America. In some real sense, the 9th Ward is Newark. The 9th Ward is South Side Chicago. The 9th Ward is neglected, abandoned urban America, Jackson said in the Times-Picayune article.

On April 15, 2007, I forwarded emails to Senators Vitter and Jindal, and Jesse Jackson. The email had a timeline and synopsis of the program and was entitled "Serious Problems within the Road Home Program." As I spoke to other Aides of political officials and received their email addresses, the same email was then forwarded to Sheila Williams of Rainbow PUSH Coalition, the local president and Regional Director of the NAACP, Senator Francis Heitmeir, Representative Jeff Arnold and his assistant, and Senator Mary Landrieu. I received a call and letter from then Senator Jindal's office regarding my concerns.

It appeared that normal hiring practices of the Road Home program were intended to place individuals in key positions that would not be able to figure out when funds were mis-appropriated. Many of the managers fostered a robotic intelligence and literally repeated what was being told to them by Virginia…word for word and not a sentence more. When the advisors and counselors asked pertinent questions regarding the program, managers almost all the time had no answers until they conferred with Virginia. When I filed my Equal Employment Opportunity Commission (EEOC) complaint, I wonder if EEOC reviewed all the applications that came in, if any, for the position that Virginia was given. According to her, she didn't have to interview for her position because she was friends with Bill. It was turning out that the Small Rental Property Program was turning into the same mismanaged fiasco as the Homeowner Assistance Program. Our office had completed Round One of applications and not one landlord had received a grant award.

In the meantime, I was moved from office to office in their continued relentless childish attempts to get rid of me. I started off in January with a great window view of the New Orleans Superdome. However, on my fourth office move, I had a window view of bricks of the empty V.A. Hospital with the loud vending machines outside my office door. Sometimes I was told to move merely one office doorway down from the office that I was currently in. Seriously? Because they hadn't come up with a way to get rid of me themselves, and all their other attempts were blunders, they were hoping that I would exit from the program on my own if they made life uncomfortable for me by taking away all of my assignments, and getting others to aid them with harassing me and slandering my name.

I received an email from my old buddy who I had originally shared offices with in Baton Rouge. He said that Bill was a "gone pecan." We often kept in touch as he too was aware of the schemes that Virginia and the others were up to. Karen, being the kiss ass that she said she was, had sided with Virginia. My old office buddy said that she was now up to three lunches a day.

As everyone was being directed to help out in Baton Rouge, when we arrived, advisors, counselors and I were shocked at what we witnessed in one room. *"Oh my God, what is that?"* *One person said. "Liiii-sa, this can't be for real Liiii-sa!"* The elder Advisor said. *"Are those applications...and documents all on the floor?"* Someone else said. There were thousands of the citizens' applications along with their confidential documentation on the floor. No wonder the applicants were being asked to send in the same document four, five and sometimes six times. Whoever was receiving them at the Baton Rouge office simply threw them on the floor. Some of the reasons they were giving applicants as to why they needed them to resend the documents was that *"it was never sent in to begin with."* Another excuse was *"it must have gotten lost in the mail."* It was lost in the mail alright! It was in the file room piled up on the floor next to the brand new file cabinets.

Some applicants were told that if they didn't resend their application and documentation they would be dropped from the program. Others were forwarded letters stating that since the Road Home program had not heard from them they would be removed from the program as well. Oftentimes messages could not be returned to anyone at the Road Home program due to the fact that their voice mail boxes were full.

In May of 2007, the Operations Manager received an email from management in Baton Rouge asking him to help out with getting rid of me and keeping me away from the employees. By now, he had apologized at least twice to me for his harassing and aggressive behavior in assisting management with their wrongdoing. He said, *"There won't be a third apology, I'm not helping them anymore…they're on their own."* He came into my office and closed the door behind him that afternoon and showed me the email. It was from the newly hired manager who had talked about how unorganized the program was when he first joined the program. You know, the Stepford Wife. This guy was telling the Operations Manager that they needed him to help out with keeping me from talking to the other employees and wanted to know if they could count on him to help them out. I thanked him for showing me the email. The Operations Manager said that he would never harass me and help them in their attempts to get rid of me again. He said that he wasn't going to be working there for long as he was going to be working with another contracted company.

SIX
WHICH APPLICANT IS FANNIE MAE?

I DIDN'T HAVE TO GO TO THE EMPLOYEES FOR information on the daily changing procedures of the program anymore; as they were now bringing information to me.

Remember the older female advisor who cried at the meeting where Waldo made those ugly remarks? She sent an email that had a 601 page document attached to it to another Advisor who then forwarded the document to me. *"Oh my God, this can't be for real! There are names of every employee who had ever worked with the Road Home program for the entire State of Louisiana."* This document was an invoice to the State for payment for the month of April of 2007. It was now June of 2007, and ICF had already received payment for the month of April. I compared my check stubs for the month of April to that document. The actual hours worked did not add up with what ICF had requested from the State for reimbursement. Were these guys double billing? And remember

Waldo's frisky ass? Well, the jury's still out on what the hell he was good at but he resigned in March of 2007 and was still on the payroll in April receiving multiple salaries. Now I had finally figured out his secret. His ass was good at payroll fraud! This dude was receiving salaries for the same billing period for titles as a Director I and Manager IV. I can't think of anyone who's getting paid multiple salaries for the same month's billing and is no longer with the company. As the character of Florida from "Good Times" would say, *"Damn, damn, damn!"* Ohh-uhh-uhh! *"Who the hell were these people? Where did they come from? And why were the citizens of New Orleans getting screwed again after losing every frickin' thing that we owned?!"*

I asked the Advisor who gave me the document who did she get the document from, as I could already see who forwarded it to her. But wanting to get it from the horse's mouth, she said she received it from another Advisor which is what the email's forward implied. The Advisor said that it was sent to her by management in Baton Rouge and that they had accidentally sent it to several of the Advisors and Counselors because they didn't know how to use the computers. Not knowing who all the email was forwarded to, and knowing that management would only lie about it as they had done in the past about everything else, I knew I had to get this document in the right hands for an unbiased review of the program, as the information contained in that document was now greater than what I had imagined.

I told Elaine about the document and she too felt that the program was clearly getting out of hand. I decided to get in touch with the District Attorney's office and schedule a meeting with Eddie Jordan. I called his office for about a week and couldn't get past his secretary without tipping my hand as to what I wanted with him. At this point, not knowing who all were in on this master scheme to profit from the City's devastation, I was very careful as to who I shared information with from there on out.

The next week as I drove down Poydras Street passing City Hall, I was stopped at the red light as people were crossing the walkway. God is good all the time! My friends always tell me I have a halo over me…and I believe they are right. Guess who was walking right in front of my car as I'm jammin' to Robin Thicke's "Lost Without You?" None other than Mr. Eddie Jordan himself! I quickly rolled down my window and said, *"Excuse me Mr. Jordan, my name is Lisa Brown and I have been trying to set up a meeting through your secretary to meet with you concerning suspicious financial activity regarding the Road Home program. I'm the Compliance Specialist for the New Orleans territory and I think you'll be interested in the documents that I have for you to review." "Please to meet you. Have her to schedule you an appointment to meet with me ASAP and tell her that I okayed it." "Thank you sir, sorry for the interruption." "Not a problem,"* he replied.

I began to prepare a meeting agenda of the things I wanted to show him and his Investigator.

While waiting for a meeting date, reports were coming in that personnel at the Baton Rouge office needed to get clarification on which applicant was Fannie Mae and a telephone number to call her back at? It was said that one of the employees had forwarded information to senior management on an applicant calling about a Fannie Mae program and the senior manager on the receiving end of that call in Baton Rouge thought that "Fannie Mae" was an actual person and not a program. Fannie Mae or the Federal National Mortgage Association (FNMA) pronounced *Fannie Mae* is a government-sponsored enterprise (GSE) in the secondary mortgage market and is one of the two largest sources of housing finance agencies in the United States. By now, I was beginning to feel like the Marilyn Munster of the bunch. Yep, these people would forever be remembered. In their calamity to set up the Road Home Program, they had to use computers, faxes, and simple technology. If they had been managers and directors in the past, they should have been used to using these types of technologies. From not knowing that they hit the "send button" on the computer to asking the intake application advisors which applicant was "Fannie Mae," they should have received awards for being complete blunders.

I received a phone call from the Stepford Wife who asked, *"Do you know how to "hide" a document in Excel?"*

Now, most people when they do reports in excel use this feature to keep from having to do the report all over again from another prospective. You see, when you have to do multiple reports, you can use some of the same information from the previous report. Instead of starting over again, you simply "hide" the column or row you don't need and keep the one's you do. Then you can add additional information on the second report so that it reflects the numbers or stats you need for a conclusive report. So hiding information can sometimes be a good thing as it saves you time on multiple reports you're working on. But when the Stepford Wife called to hide documents, oftentimes it was not to create a good or reflective report of what was happening in the program. It was to create a diversion so that the reader of the report could think that certain activities were being performed when, on the contrary, they were not. *"What are you trying to do?"* I asked. *"I want to hide the zip codes."*

Newspaper Article
The Road Home run-around

"I called my Road Home resolution team supervisor (my 14th) for days and left messages on the phone number he gave me. The recording says you reached the extension, but the extension has no name for that mailbox.

When I called their Baton Rouge main switchboard, I got "the operator is not available."

When I called the "Road to La" 888 call center, I got "we can't transfer calls."

When I called the automated directory to find my supervisor's extension, I got "no one by that name works here."

When he finally called me back, he said he doesn't check his voice mail.

I have been in Stage 5 Verification and Resolution for six months. Benefits calculated means nothing if those benefit letters have not been made available to the applicants. Benefits calculated means nothing if those letters went out wrong. They skew their numbers to project perceived performance.

Is it time for a lawsuit yet?" one concerned applicant stated in the Times-Picayune.

Elaine had told me that she went out with the Rehab Inspectors and that management from Baton Rouge had given them a report with 10 properties on them to inspect. Elaine went on to say, *"That tour was a mess!"* *"What?! Girl what happened?"* I asked curiously. *"Many of the homes that we went to look at either did not exist and the zip codes were not zip codes in New Orleans."* One home that they visited was no longer there, yet it had already been approved to get funds. The report stated that the contracted appraisers actually went into this "invisible" home that nobody saw to inspect the property. Elaine said, *"I tried to keep a copy of the report and even put it in my purse, but they wouldn't let us out the vehicle unless we turned everything back in to them."* Also, *"the names of the owners of the homes that were being questioned were conveniently left off. I tell you it was just a complete mess."*

By now the Operations Manager had resigned and left the program. After he decided to not assist management in Baton Rouge with their mission to get rid of me, his duties were limited.

There were so many managers to come through the Road Home program that I had lost count and couldn't keep up anymore.

SEPT
THE AGENDA

I SLOWLY BEGAN TO CRACK THE SECRET IN MY ATTEMPT to figure out why tens of thousands of individuals were not being helped and why the program was being intentionally delivered at a snail's pace.

When a grant Agreement is awarded from HUD, there is an executed timeline to meet and either HUD or the State will monitor the recipient of that contract and hold the company accountable for any program delivery activities that are not being carried out in a timely manner.

In the meantime, I had been given my meeting date with District Attorney Jordan and had completed my meeting agenda of the concerns I wanted to discuss with them.

I gave District Attorney Jordan and his Investigator a Meeting Agenda that I prepared and discussed each item in order. I then turned over the 601 page document. I had already flagged the pages that I wanted to talk about and showed him where Waldo was receiving multiple salaries. I explained to both of them that Waldo was no longer with the company. I showed him my check stubs and what the contracted company had calculated on the document to be my time worked for the month of April. My actual check stub and the figures on the document were not congruent. They both knew something was wrong. Because of limited funding for his department to do a thorough investigation of a program of that magnitude, Attorney Jordan contacted the State Auditor regarding our concerns. His department also put in a call to the FBI (Lakefront Division) and told me that someone would be contacting me shortly.

It appeared that everyone had their own agenda. It was discovered that the Army Corps of Engineers had built faulty levees and in their present efforts to repair the damage, they were cutting costs and corners again by repairing them with newspaper. While the citizens of the Greater New Orleans area were attempting to get their lives back on track, the public school educational system was still in shambles.

As the person that monitors federal grants programs for over 10 years, every company, including the one I currently work for has always listened to my guidance regarding procedures, trainings, and waivers to alleviate the possible fining of millions of dollars in the future. This particular company; however, had another agenda.

While the entire world watched in amazement the recovery efforts take place in the Greater New Orleans area, I was witnessing a chilling account of another disaster developing right before my eyes while on the inside. I wasn't just the compliance expert; I was a victim myself, in that I had lost every single possession as a homeowner too. I was completely devoted to making this program run efficiently. I rang the alarm so many times, that my responsibilities were demoted, my office moved four times, and my hair falling out from all the emotional abuse that I endured from directors and managers. I was beginning to wonder if it was sheer human nature for people to take advantage of things and people when a tragedy happens.

Meanwhile, the following attachment in an email was sent to everyone who worked for the Road Home program.

The
Road Home

BUILDING A SAFER,
STRONGER, SMARTER LOUISIANA

BOMB THREAT CHECKLIST

Exact time of call

_____

Exact words of caller

_____

QUESTIONS TO ASK

1. When is the bomb going to explode?
2. Where is the bomb?
3 What does it look like?
4. What kind of bomb is it?
5. What will cause it to explode?
6. Did you place the bomb?
7. Why?
8. Where are you calling from?
9. What is your address?
10. What is your name?

CALLERS VOICE (circle)

Calm	Disguised	Nasal	Angry	Broken
Stutter	Slow	Sincere	Lisp	Rapid
Giggling	Deep	Crying	Squeaky	Excited
Stressed	Accent	Loud	Slurred	Normal

If voice is familiar, whom did it sound like?

_____

Were there any background noises?

_____

Remarks:

_____

Person receiving call:

_____

Telephone number call received at:

_____

Date:

_____

Report call immediately to:

_____

(Refer to bomb plan incident)

_____

In the event of a bomb threat, please contact the police officer in your facility, and have you manager notify one of the following

Craig Bolling, Director of Security
Ann Broderick, Shaw Security, Manager
Office: 225-242-1012 / 225-231-1350
Mobile: 225-247-6261

These are questions that a Special Weapons And Tactics (SWAT) team should ask. However, this was an email that was sent out to us in August of 2007. Did ICF really think that any employee would ask these questions if someone called to say that there's a bomb in the workplace? You tell your superior and get the hell out of there…and call the police on your way out the door!!! Did someone really make a threat to our offices? Was it Fannie Mae?

With their lack of concern for some of the citizens and how they handled the program, we're lucky we all got out alive. And to think that they were worried about people bringing guns. Well, with a bomb threat, they didn't have that worry anymore. Now they'd gone and pissed somebody off. They brought their pompous attitudes to our city and now someone was threatening to blow up the joint! The bomb had already gone off in the workplace. The way the program was being run, it was doomed for disaster.

To think they couldn't run the Road Home program and now they thought they could take on a potential person with an explosive device! I could see it now, *"Please hold on Miss Fannie Mae, I need to find out if Mr. Bomber is "sincere" and "normal."* Clearly these people weren't the *normal* ones; however, they were *sincere* in their efforts to not make the program work.

So I googled "Bomb Threat Checklist" and guessed what popped up? We had received an identical version of another company's bomb threat checklist almost word for word as the one that was distributed to us.

http://www.dm.usda.gov/physicalsecurity/bombthreat.htm

Shaw or ICF probably got paid a hefty penny to develop this *Bomb Threat Checklist* than the award amount that the applicant's who applied with the program to get their homes repaired got. What was missing with the Road Home's checklist was a *local* name and number of who to contact. It would have been nice to receive the names and numbers of the police officers in our facility as the document states to contact those individuals. But what could you expect. At least we got something. I guess after we ran around looking for the police officer we could then *"have **you** manager notify one of the following"* as it's written at the bottom of the document which then references the Director of Security or Shaw's Security Manager. Since they were located in Baton Rouge which is 90 miles away from our offices, hopefully by the time it took them to get to New Orleans we'd still be alive.

August and September were pretty slow months, as the Small Rental Property program's employees were not given many assignments. Our staff members were now being asked to help out with the first program, as we were told that there were no landlords applying anymore for assistance.

Then four Caucasian boys who appeared to be in their late teens or early 20's came in and started giving direction.

All communications from and to our Baton Rouge office was halted. They too lacked supervisory skills. They were very careful in interacting and communicating with the employees and management in Baton Rouge would not give clear answers as to whether or not these boys were supervisors. *"Where's the fax machine?"* one of them asked. *"You're standing next to it!"* an Advisor yelled out. *"How do you put paper in it to receive a fax,"* he then asked. Everyone started laughing. Lord here we go again! We all thought we were being punked. These young boys stayed on their cell phone a lot as if they were getting direction from someone else. Who that person was, we will never know. I would never find out what their agenda was as my time would soon come to an end.

HUIT
IF YOU SAY IT ENOUGH,
THEY'LL BELIEVE IT

ON SEPTEMBER 13, 2007, I WAS TERMINATED AS FOUR Caucasian men, who refused to show identification, came into my office while two of them closed my office door and stood outside so that no one could get in. One of them thuggishly pointed his fingers in my face and told me that he would make certain that I would never get employed anywhere else again. The day before, I responded to an important email that was forwarded to me. At the time, management in Baton Rouge didn't know that the person who I was telling to contact the governor and their local politicians to alert them about the program's mismanagement was my father who was seeking assistance from the HAP program, the program for single-unit homeowners. He wanted to get the name and number of the employee he had been calling for three months, and like so many other citizens, most applicants were getting the run around.

RE: Information

9/12/07

Reply▼

Brown, Lisa

LBrown@Road2LA.org

Add to contacts

To: Omitted

From: Brown, Lisa (LBrown@Road2LA.org)

Sent: Wed 9/12/07 8:40 AM

Her email address is *XXXXX@road2la.org*. You are wasting your time in your attempts to contact this young lady if you have been contacting her for months and she has not responded, she will NOT respond to your email. I would suggest that you contact (through certified mail) your State Rep and the Governor's office and show them what documents you have been turning in regarding your insurance claims that no one with the Road Home want to acknowledge, as there is being an assignment that the Small Rental Program employees have been asked to assist with with the Homeowners Program. This special assignment will only be for three days…today, tomorrow and Friday. It was supposed to take place all week; however, as usual, nothing was set in place for the week's assignment to be a success. In other words, it will already…inevitably fail. Something that

I gather, just from previous works, it was intended to do. This special project is called UP60 Project. I forget what the acronym is for. They all have special sounds and sayings but the end result is that no one gets any professional, useful assistance.

We have been given the task to call people who have applied with the Homeowners Program (that would be you) who have ALLEGEDLY not responded to The Road Home. We are suppose to tell these homeowners that we need them to PREFERABLY fax (not come in to the office) documents needed to complete their applications since The Road Home program has ALLEGEDLY not heard from them in over 60 days. These instructions came from someone named XXXXX XXXXXXXXX who is over the Homeowners Program on the 9th floor at the Poydras location at (504) 584-1674. She is also over several other branch locations of the 1st program. Although she indicated that this is a trial test just for this week only, once again, it doesn't seem like much thought has been put into the project. They have hired five new employees to head this project for the ALLEGEDLY one week, in which many of them on yesterday could not even access the computer and struggled with how to retrieve paper from the fax machine. We DID NOT do any work again on yesterday and received an email stating that we will begin doing work today so now we have to squeeze in calling over 400 homeowners in three days and request that they bring in documentation that they ALLEGEDLY never brought in in over 60 days.

I suspect that whether phone calls are made or not, if you are one of those homeowners on this list, hundreds of homeowners will not be receiving assistance and this will be the reason(s) used to *justify* The Road Home not delving out any monies. *"We attempted to contact you…but you didn't answer your phone or we requested that documentation be faxed to us but you didn't fax it."* Whatever the reason, the bottom line is you will not get any monies. At this point, I wouldn't trust anything unless I certified it through the mail to these people.

Regards,
Zelia 'Lisa' Brown
Compliance Division
ICF International
1555 Poydras Street, Suite 752
New Orleans, Louisiana 70112
(504) 584-1668 (local office)
(504) 584-1781 (facsimile)
ZBrown@icfi.com
LBrown@road2la.org

⚜ ⚜ ⚜

I guess you could tell my frustration at this point. As the Compliance Specialist for the New Orleans area, it was clear that there was nothing that I could do to turn things around for the better. All hope and confidence for management to do what they should have been doing to assist the public was gone. Upon citing federal irregularities, and huge procedural conflicts to the company that received the contract, I began to be repeatedly left out of major meetings, harassed, discriminated against, abandoned, and eventually fired. That was ICF's agenda from the beginning when they realized that I wasn't going to be a mere token and that it was my intention to perform the job that I was hired to do. As Martin Luther King once said, *"Injustice anywhere is a threat to justice everywhere."*

After losing my home of 15 years, fighting with insurance companies on what my policy said I should get due to the loss, paying attorney's fees to get what I knew I should have gotten to begin with, fighting Countrywide for holding on to a $50,000 check, and being fired from the Road Home program after alerting federal authorities of alleged financial fraud; if it weren't for my faith in God, and the undying support of my family and close friends, I would be emotionally ruined.

You cannot take money from one federal program to pay another. Having reviewed HUD contracts for quite some time now with various County, State, City, non-profit, and for profit entities, I've never found a contract to be written of that nature. You could possibly add another line item in your reporting system or place comments in the Disaster Recovery Grant Reporting (DRGR) system, but if the company that received the grant to run the Road Home program had to resort to that 'after' the fact, then that tells me that the contract was not an air-tight Agreement from the very beginning. It should have been considering that this program was the most that any one company has ever received in the history of America. This would explain why all the chaos happened and not one person be held accountable. In other words, the Agreement, that had to be signed by extremely high officials at the U.S. Department of Housing and Urban Development (HUD), Office of Community Development (OCD), Louisiana Recovery Authority (LRA), the State, and ICF, all knew that this binding contractual Agreement would be equivalent to that of "taking candy from a baby" without proper and adequate deadlines, timeframes, demands, etc. And everyone involved in obtaining a contract through the program (Grantees and Sub-grantees) would be the richest people on the planet Earth after the contract ends two years later. While one may rob Peter to pay Paul in one's personal finances or home life; when it comes to spending federal dollars, it may be viewed as criminal conduct and intent and may constitute a HUD/OIG audit. With everyone's hand in the cookie jar, the citizens of New Orleans didn't have a standing chance to recover.

Directing employees from the Small Rental Property program to perform duties with the first program, the Housing Assistance Program that has another account, different directors, different delivery line items and administrative funds should not have happened. If the directors and managers had ever managed federally funded programs previously, this would be common knowledge to them. In other words, you cannot use the budget from the Small Rental Property program to pay for delivery items provided by the Homeowner Assistance Program and vice versa.

I truly believe that what you put out you get back…good or bad.

Some companies put a spin on things and situations to create a diversion to make them look like they are the good guys and you're the villain. Their mission should have read, *"If you say it enough, they will believe it."* So the spin that was put on me was "Let's say she's dumb and lacks luster. Let's say she didn't know how to perform her job duties. Let's say she stole something." These stereotypes are unfortunately placed on many whistleblowers every day so that the public will not believe the truth. They felt that if they said it enough someone would believe it and hopefully it would catch on like wildfire so that whatever information and documents I turned in to authorities would be questioned. They wanted to get the magnifying glass off them and placed on me. They knew that the public on the outside viewed them in a negative light already, and if someone from the inside concurred and was the Compliance expert for the program too, it would not look good for them. But because people had eagerly befriended *me* and because of my character, many employees from both programs had already witnessed the berating that management had done by pitting one against the other. Mind controlling games to keep people in their place became an everyday occurrence.

Not even one week after being terminated (without a verbal reason why or a "pink slip" stating the reason why), I received a call on my cell from a ranking police officer with the New Orleans Police Department (NOPD) telling me that he had something for me that he felt I may be interested in. If it weren't for this gentleman, I would have never known that this company had gone from being slanderous to being libel by defaming my name, character, and pristine reputation. They were now telling employees that I had stolen applicants Social Security Numbers and was selling them for $50 dollars each. In the position that I was in as Compliance Specialist, I never came in contact with applicants. I strictly dealt with program's guidelines and timeframes and the directors who were implementing the program.

To put the nail in the coffin, ICF placed an 8½ x 11 sheet of paper on the 1st, 7th, and 9th floors of a headshot picture of me, in color, in the Poydras building that they were leasing. When this Sergeant gave me a copy of myself, and I'm looking at my picture and the caption on the paper, it reminded me of the pictures that one sees in the Post Office of wanted felons. I knew then that I needed to obtain legal help to get this terrifying company to cease with the blatant discriminatory tactics and defamation of my character and reputation. The Sergeant said that out of all the Caucasians that had been fired, I was the *only* one they chose to place pictures of in the building as they gave out confidential information regarding my personnel records letting everyone know that I had been terminated. They had made sure that no one knew about Waldo's HR situation. He went on to say, *"It's a complete violation of not only your personnel records, but your human rights. In all my years, I've never seen anything like this; you're such a great person."*

The
Road Home

BUILDING A SAFER,
STRONGER, SMARTER LOUISIANA

Zelia "Lisa" Brown

If this former employee is seen at this facility, Craig Bolling, Director of Security and Safety, should be contacted immediately at 225.247.6261.

If you noticed the signature title for the **Bomb Threat Checklist** that Mr. Bolling or HR sent out in August of 2007, his title was Director of Security. However, for my picture that was posted and blasted on the 1st, 7th and 9th floors for all entrants to see, the word "Safety" was purposely added in September of 2007. Another created diversion to give the reader the impression that they may not be *safe* if I am ever in the building…a building mind you that ICF did not own. It was a scare tactic and an outright exaggeration of who I am. These directors and managers used their abusive power to harass, slander, and defame me in the workplace in front of my peers, and in public places.

Who gave these people this much power? It was like pouring salt on an opened wound…and there were hundreds of boxes of salt left to pour as they laughed and schemed.

NEWS ARTICLE

Paul Gates Investigates: ICF

Posted Nov 16, 2007 09:56 AM CST

A lawsuit filed against ICF, the company hired to distribute relief money for victims of hurricanes Katrina and Rita, alleges the company triple-billed the state, deliberately misled victims, and handed out money for properties that did not exist.

The woman who filed the suit, once worked for ICF. She came to the job with impressive credentials. But once she says she began noticing wrongdoing, and reporting it, she was shown the door....

NOT QUALIFIED

IT HAD BEEN THREE YEARS SINCE KATRINA. BEING blackballed from obtaining employment from 2008 to 2009 because I was a whistleblower was not exciting. My daughters and I moved back to Houston.

Gas prices were starting to go up and more and more people were beginning to lose their jobs. The national debt had the biggest increase than any president in U.S. history under President George Bush, according to White House Correspondent for CBS News Mark Knoller.

Now looking for work became more competitive with more qualified people looking as well. I had applied for hundreds of jobs and had also frequented temporary agencies where I would take clerical tests with overall software skills and computer scores in the high 90's and typing 74 wpm.

In June of 2008, Mortgage News Daily announced that attorney generals of California, Illinois, and the Washington State department that regulated financial institutions all filed lawsuits against Countrywide alleging "variations on the theme of mortgage fraud." Time classified Angelo Mozilo as one of the "25 People to Blame for the Financial Crisis" in their article regarding "…greed behind the meltdown." Wow! I knew this was coming. Finally, some good news! I warned them in my letter last year about this. If only they had listened.

Afterwards, I obtained an interview and received a job offer paying extremely less than what I normally make. I took the job anyway because I knew that eventually I could move up the ladder because of my skill sets and taking on additional responsibilities. This agency though, had similar mind-sets that were synonymous with individuals from the Road Home program. These directors and managers appeared to be unfamiliar with federal housing procedure and terminology. One Division Manager, in his quest to fit in, would use malapropisms in sentences (an unintentionally humorous misuse or distortion of a word that is substituted for other words with similar sounds), thinking that it would make him sound intelligent. And what do you know. There was another Waldo in the building…same age…just more pathetic. Oh my God, could this be déjà vu?

With great admiration, Senator Barack Obama was just elected as President of the United States to take over and fix some of the worse 'shiggity' passed down to any president in history, given the economic times and crisis.

No sooner than I had completed assisting with an Executive Summary and a five year housing plan with the agency, I was given a pink slip which stated I was, "*...unable or unwilling to render satisfactory service... and grossly misrepresented her proficiency level around technology, analytical and interpersonal skills during the interview screening process.*"

Unbeknownst to the agency, one of the ranking employees pulled me over to the side and gave me a three page document that ICF's attorney's had mailed to them two weeks before I was let go. The letter from ICF's attorney's stated that I was the Plaintiff involved in a federal lawsuit and was asking them for my personnel records from the agency regarding my work there for the past 2 months that I had been employed.

In their ploy to possibly cover up their own agendas, they had no idea that only a month ago, I had successfully taken a clerical and technology test with an independent temporary agency which contradicted everything they said about me in the termination letter. Who knows, maybe ICF encouraged them to say that so they could try to build a case with another agency. When will companies like this ever learn?

I knew there was something wrong. The last couple of weeks of my employment with that agency just didn't feel right. I wouldn't put it past ICF if they had additional verbal conversations with my employer, as they too were in hot water with HUD and had to "repay back $15.5 million to settle findings that it misspent grants from three federal housing programs." It would be the most money that any organization has had to repay a federal entity in America's history. It's pretty difficult to misspend $15 million. While these people were encouraged to terminate me because of their similar circumstances, it was evident that they too were not qualified to run a federal housing program. After reading news reports of their blatant mismanagement of federal dollars, I began to understand why they would lie about my job performance to justify my termination. They, too, were used to wrongdoing.

I was on that job for less than 90 days. Was there any company left that followed the law around here?

I would learn later that not only did ICF's attorney's forward the letter to the company that fired me, but they were sending out numerous letters to all the companies that I had been attempting to gain employment with.

I then contacted my attorney again.

Why can't I get over Katrina?

Meanwhile, ICF was going through another lawsuit where former Advisors were contending that ICF's refusal to pay overtime to employees enabled them "to reap millions of dollars in wage savings." Employees were alleging that ICF had overworked and underpaid them. Labor department investigators concluded the company "improperly labeled employees as administrators," which would exempt them from obtaining overtime pay as mandated by the Fair Labor Standards Act.

September 24, 2010, the NAACP Legal Defense and Educational Fund represented more than 20,000 African-American homeowners and two fair housing organizations to win an injunction "protecting funds from the Road Home Program so that displaced homeowners can have an opportunity to show that Louisiana and HUD have distributed recovery funds in a discriminatory manner."

FOOD STAMPS (Part II)

WITH THE UNEMPLOYMENT RATE AT 9.6 PERCENT AND rising, and I being a part of that number, I dropped my daughters off to school and applied for Food Stamps. I had no more savings and my 401K was depleted.

As I walked in the agency, one woman whispered to the other one sitting next to her, *"Girl you know it must be pretty bad out there if somebody lookin' like her needs assistance." "Umm Hmm, I like her purse,"* the other woman said.

I sat down in the only empty chair left, filled out the application, and waited for hours for my name to be called.

Continuing to apply for employment, I landed a job back in my field as grants monitor and compliance specialist doing the exact same thing that ICF had been blocking me doing. My agency is the funding source to multiple sub-recipients receiving funds from President Obama's American Recovery and Reinvestment Act (ARRA) and Housing and Economic Recovery Act (HERA). With all the housing programs that I am over, I make sure that agencies are legally spending their monies in which I am over a combined total budget of $3.4M of federal funds from HUD. I was able to go right in and start the programs from scratch, provide training to directors and staff members, and partner with well known agencies like Habitat for Humanity. I also received accolades and recognition from HUD in 2010 for *"meeting expenditure deadlines ahead of schedule,"* an undertaking that ICF failed to accomplish with their contract to run the Road Home Program.

NEUF
STARTING OVER

PROGRESS IS DEFINED AS ADVANCEMENT, IMPROVEMENT, or to move forward. The real decision makers of the Road Home program had preconceived stereotypes of how the locals and the citizens of New Orleans were. Because of this, the laws to disburse money to the citizens of New Orleans were grossly different than the way money was distributed in Mississippi. As a result, it was impossible for the citizens to progress at the degree that they should have given the fact that billions of dollars were pumped into the City.

The issuance of those funds set a clear precedence for chaos and set the stage for discrimination on all levels. Being allowed to tell a homeowner that they "don't qualify for road home funds" and then turn around and tell that same homeowner, "I'll buy your home for a little of nothing" was the highest level of disrespect and an overall conflict of interest.

Five years later, more information is being divulged and federal decisions are being rendered that would hopefully improve future disaster recovery efforts.

With 11 federal lawsuits against the contracted company, and counting, this alone exhibits a greater need for serious investigations regarding disaster recovery as a whole and how contracts are awarded, as it does not eviscerate the facts of what was happening on the inside concerning the self-serving leadership and multiple financial improprieties.

Susan L. Taylor once said, *"In every crisis there is a message. Crises are nature's way of forcing change--breaking down old structures, shaking loose negative habits so that something new and better can take their place."* From my personal crisis of losing everything, and repeatedly being blocked by ICF to obtain job security and make a living for myself and family, I knew I had to do something. *"I had to make my own living and my own opportunity...."* – Madame C. J. Walker.

Forcing change, breaking down old stereotypes, and embarking upon positive transformations is something that every citizen of New Orleans should strive for. We should never give up and should always question people when they demand our silence.

Five years later, residents are still living in shell shot houses, homes that don't have roofs, electricity, or unsanitary plumbing.

Mentally ill patients and individuals must be arrested and go to jail in order to obtain needed medication as the mental hospitals and facilities are not back up and running. Charity hospital, the only public hospital still today remains closed.

The homeless population has doubled. Many of the elderly (60 plus years old) are still living in a FEMA trailer. Come January 1, 2011, residents who have trailers will receive a hefty *daily* fine, if they do not remove the trailers from in front of their uninhabitable home.

If you calculate the number of households in New Orleans; then add the number of persons living inside of those households who are 18 years and older; each household recipient could have been awarded $150,000 each and there would still be millions of dollars left to give back to the federal government considering the sizeable grant amount that ICF received to disburse to the public. Nevertheless, New Orleans, in many areas, is still on life support.

The Small Rental Property Program did not bring back "reasonably priced rental properties in the most storm damaged areas" as it promised it would. Instead, rental housing has risen to astronomical numbers in the Greater New Orleans area compared to other surrounding States. HUD's survey shows that there are "significant increases in the cost of housing, especially for lower and middle-income renters."

According to U.S. Housing and Urban Development Secretary Shaun Donovan, the *2009 New Orleans Metropolitan Area Housing Survey* exhibited a "startling picture of just how disruptive Hurricane Katrina was to the lives of tens of thousands of families throughout the New Orleans area."

In spite of the negative news reports, the company that received the contract to run the Road Home program, ICF, still receives housing grants from HUD and other federal agencies.

The U.S. Navy, the Department of Health and Human Services, U.S. Environmental Protection Agency, National Institute of Health (NIH), Federal Highway Administration, and the U.S. Department of Education have all awarded prime contracts to ICF.

HUD alone has awarded ICF over $15.7 million on March 5, 2010 with a five-year re-compete award.

Katrina has triggered numerous questions that have yet to be answered. *Where did the money go, as most of it did not reach the New Orleans residents? What has happened to the multiple lawsuits in federal court regarding the contracted company? Why hasn't anyone from the previous administration been held accountable? What are the solutions moving forward?*

And the million dollar question is, *"Why is the company that received the contract to ruin (no typo here) the Road Home program still obtaining large grant awards from HUD and other federal agencies?"*

Starting over Alex and Torey remain vigilant learners as Alex became recipient of the Provost Undergraduate Research Scholarship (PURS) award at the University of Houston, and made the Dean's List while Torey became the first African-American president at Pin Oak middle school in Bellaire, Texas, vice-president of the National Junior Honor Society, and is one of the youngest members of the So Real Dance Cru.

As for me, in addition to supervising HUD programs, I started The Brown Foundation, Inc. which provides free books to children from birth to five in the Greater New Orleans area to empower children as only 38% of Black males in New Orleans graduate from high school. The school system five years later still suffers from low standards and expectations.

I started my own resume writing service in which I've helped numerous people get jobs when they had previously struggled with obtaining employment in the corporate sector prior to obtaining *my* services.

I've helped countless people obtain stable employment with the Federal government by strategically marketing the applicant on paper and targeting their skill sets. I direct them and give advisement on how to navigate the federal jobs website. I also give them pointers on how to increase their overall score. I knew something was wrong when others who I had done resumes for were getting jobs and I wasn't! At the time, it just didn't make sense. I'm also in the midst of developing intellectual property.

On a personal note, Juan and I reconnected again but for whatever reasons have not been able to make it better the second time around. They say there's always one who you will never forget and who will always have your heart; that would be Juan. One day my Juan will come.

In order for this great City to rise again, the government must learn the lessons of Hurricane Katrina. Studies show that *disaster relief efforts* cost 15 times more than being proactive. Albert Einstein's insanity theorem talks about expecting different results by doing the same thing over and over again.

As a race that has been fractured, divided, and sold, we are now forced to deal with gentrification which allows some residents not to be able to leave ANYTHING to their offspring, as it relates to the American dream and homeownership.

While we define our rights as individuals, we (Blacks, Whites, Technicolor), must work together in order to build and gain sustainability. Some critics seem to think that it wasn't necessarily 'racism' but 'classism' that took place post Katrina. *To-may-toes...to-mah-toes,* discrimination in any medium is just that. While Katrina claimed more than 1,800 lives on the Gulf Coast, and over $125 Billion in damages, one can clearly see that this unfortunate devastation was an equal opportunity storm. The recovery efforts; however, was not.

The name "Hurricane Katrina" has been retired by the World Meteorological Organization's hurricane committee since it was an unusually large and damaging hurricane. According to the committee, "using it again could be considered insensitive." As for the residents of City of New Orleans, that's "awsom" news!

This book is dedicated to all those who lost their lives and to their loved ones who remain in limbo during the aftermath of Hurricane Katrina; whether by body or in mind.

[28]"Come to me, all you who are weary and burdened, and I will give you rest. [29]Take my yoke upon you and learn from me, for I am gentle and humble in heart, and you will find rest for your souls. [30]For my yoke is easy and my burden is light." Matthew 11: 28-30

Zelia Elise Brown is founder and chief executive officer of The Brown Foundation, Inc. (TBF) which is a not for profit organization that provides free books to children from birth to five years of age in the Greater New Orleans area and surrounding parishes to combat illiteracy, as Louisiana ranks #2 in the nation. AT&T and Target have partnered with TBF. Brown is also owner of Write On Target, a professional resume writing service that specializes in executive and federal employment where her business has been impactful nationwide in helping clients receive employment in the corporate sector as well as the federal government with the department of the V.A., H.H.S., and S.S.A., to name a few. Brown assisted with the Gulf Coast rebuilding after Hurricanes Katrina and Rita, and was also a victim, herself, who lost her home (of 15 years) on the Lakefront due to the devastation of Hurricane Katrina. This Rockefeller Fellows Finalist has helped plan/develop over $877 million in housing and economic development projects in Louisiana and Texas, and has received accolades and recognition from HUD for *"meeting expenditure deadlines ahead of schedule."* Presently Brown supervises HUD programs developed from President Obama's American Recovery and Reinvestment Act, and the Housing and Economic Recovery Acts.

Brown has volunteered for Junior Achievement in Houston and is also a former Court Appointed Special Advocate (CASA) New Orleans Volunteer. Brown also formerly volunteered for the Girl Scouts of America for both the Southeast Region and San Jacinto Council for over eight years. She is a Contributing Writer for the New Orleans Agenda and is a member of several organizations such as the Louisiana Association of Nonprofit Organizations, Texas Association of Nonprofit Organizations, Algiers Economic Development Foundation, and Alpha Kappa Alpha Sorority, Incorporated.

In recognition of her leadership and achievements, Brown was nominated for the L'Oreal Paris 2008 Women of Worth Award, featured in Ebony magazine in 2007, recipient of the 2001 African-Americans in Higher Education Award (placing second in the State), a noted consultant on nonprofit organizations and numerous HUD programs such as Community Development Block Grant funds, HOME Investment Partnerships Program, HOPWA, Neighborhood Stabilization Program, Homelessness Prevention & Rapid Re-housing Program, First-time Homebuyers Program, 203K, Neighborhood Housing Improvement Funds, and former Advisor and Equal Opportunity Manager for the City of New Orleans.

A graduate of Dillard University and Dean's List student, Brown finished college in three years, holds a Bachelor of Arts degree, and went on to continue her graduate studies in Education. She is the mother of two daughters, the oldest who is recipient of the Provost Undergraduate Research Scholarship

Award (PURS) at the University of Houston, Vice-President of The Brown Foundation, Executive Assistant at Hadassah, and Research Assistant for the federal government with Veterans Administration who entered college at 17 years old with 16 college credits. Her youngest was the first African-American president of Pin Oak Middle School in Bellaire, Texas, teen advisor of The Brown Foundation, Vice-President of the National Junior Honor Society, member of Who's Who Among All-American Scholars, United States Achievement Academy, Who's Who in Student Council, featured as Student of the Week on KPRC Channel 2 News from December 21st -25th 2009, former member of So Real Dance Cru, and guitar student at Cinco Ranch Conservatory of Music. Her youngest is also featured as the *"face"* of one of the advertisements on the famous St. Charles Avenue Trolley Car (Streetcar) No. 914 in New Orleans, Louisiana, and entering honor student at Mirabeau B. Lamar High School, an International Baccalaureate World School.

For more information visit *www.brownfoundationinc. org* and *www.writeontargetresumes.com.*

ENDORSEMENT

In her breezy biography of Hurricane Katrina and its aftermath, Zelia Williams has written an amazing insider's guide to the management of the Louisiana Road Home Program for Hurricane Katrina homeowners and rental owners. Here is a tiny sample:

p. 89 *"...at each citywide workshop, these [Road Home Program] counselors were given direction to specifically say that they "could not give advice or provide direction" to the citizens seeking assistance with their application process."*

Ms. Williams does not exaggerate about ICF International's disdain for the applicants as tens of thousands of hurricane victims can describe and as noted by Times-Picayune editor Jarvis Deberry, who wrote that *"The Road Home has messed over so many people in so many ways over such a long period of time that, at this point, it takes a particularly egregious error to attract attention now."*

http://blog.nola.com/jarvisdeberry/2008/10/lose the attitude not the pape.html

– Melanie Ehrlich, Ph.D.

Founder, Citizens' Road Home Action Team (CHAT)

http://chatushome.com

04/26/2011

Carlisle said, *"No lie can live forever."* William Cullen Bryant said, *"Truth, crushed to the earth, shall rise again."* I would like to thank Zelia Williams for having the courage to speak truth to power. The local and national news media have done everything under God's sun to suppress the truth around Hurricane Katrina. Billions of dollars have come into this city, and to date, there's no proof of who received and spent the money.

– Carl Galmon

President, LA Committee Against Apartheid

04/23/2011